The Art (

How To Spot And Stop Manipulation

By

Patrick Stinson

Table of Contents

Introduction......................................8

Chapter 1: Identify If You Are The Victim Of Manipulation 10

Are You A Victim Of Manipulation?......................10

Someone Got You To Do Something You Didn't Want To..11

You Feel Guilty 12

Passive Aggressive Behavior 14

You Are Never Right................................15

You Feel Insane 17

Receiving The Silent Treatment 18

Forgive Yourself 19

Chapter 2: Why Manipulators Manipulate 21

The No Communication Skills Types......................21

How To Spot These Manipulators........................22

The Low Self-Esteem Types 24

How To Spot The Low Self-Esteem Type..............29

How To Handle Low Self-Esteem Types 34

The Controlling Types 37

How To Deal With Controlling Types 39

The Co-Dependent Types 40

How To Spot These Types 41

How To Handle Co-Dependent Types..................43

Vindictive Types...............................45

How To Handle Vindictive Types 47

The Dark Triad Types 49

How To Handle Dark Triad Types.....................53

Chapter 3: Beating The Vicious Cycle Of Manipulation 56

Use Logic Instead Of Emotion When Making A

Decision 57

Just Say No 60

Ask For Clear Terms And More Time 63

Leaving A Manipulator 65

Healing From Mental And Emotional Abuse........69

Chapter 4: How To Confront A Manipulator 73

Don't Take On Battles You Can't Win 73

Don't Be Accusational Or Emotional.....................74

Stay On Topic 77

Present Evidence If You Can..............................77

Accept That You May Not Win 78

What To Do When A Manipulator Escalates 80

Chapter 5: How To Weaken A Manipulator 85

Keep Repeating The Question 85

Show Him Hard Evidence 86

Walk Away 87

See The Game For What It Is 87

Chapter 6: Specific Considerations For Manipulation In The Working Environment 89

The Power Struggle.......................................89

Triangulation 93

Being Conditioned To Accept Harassment 97

Being Manipulated By A Client 99

Being Manipulated By Your Boss 103

Chapter 7: Specific Considerations For Manipulation 106

In Other Areas Of Life...106

Family..106

The Guilt Trip 108

Refusing Accountability....................................109

Avoid Triangulation 111

Find Allies 112

Break The Patterns 113

Stop Going To Functions That Weaken You 115

Use Your Own Persuasion 116

Refuse To Be An Enabler 117

When The Parent-Child Relationship Is Reversed

....121

Romantic Relationships.......................................123

Reaction Formation And Validating Emotions ...123

Molding Reality...126

Pressure Liars Into The Truth 128

Set Boundaries 129

Don't Permit Social Isolation 131

Confront Passive-Aggressive Behavior Head-On 133

End Rumor Spreading..135

Don't Allow Ex Smearing 136

Allow Some Dominance 137

Friendships 138

Don't Fall For The Victim Game.........................140

Watch Out For Fairweather Friends 140

Watch Out For Gossips.....................................141

Don't Do Too Many Favors 142

The Friend Who Flakes 143

Chapter 8: How To Stop Being Manipulated By Money 144

Is It Worth It?..144

Be Financially Sound Alone 146

Refuse Gifts 146

Be Private About Money.....................................147

Don't Let Money Keep You In A Horrid Job 148

Chapter 9: No Contact And Preventing Manipulation Right Off The Bat 150

Prove You're Not A Victim 150

Just Walk Away..150

The True Meaning Of No Contact.......................152

Conclusion 155

References 159

Disclaimer **163**

Introduction

Have you been the victim of manipulation? Or are you suspicious that you are a victim now? No one likes being manipulated, but with this book, you will learn how to spot, shut down, and counter manipulators.

There are a surprisingly high number of manipulators in the world. Chances are, you have been the victim of one at least once in your life. While some manipulation is inherent to human relationships, the chronic manipulators and emotional abusers are the ones who can cause you a lot of heartache.

Learning how to identify manipulators and their tactics is the first rule of engagement. The next is to shut down and say no. If the manipulator switches tactics or escalates, then you can beat him at his own game using techniques covered in this book.

You will also learn how to end relationships with manipulators and heal from their harm. It is possible to love a person who is manipulative. It can hurt a lot when you break ties, but it is necessary for your own sanctity.

Without manipulators wreaking havoc in your life, you will enjoy much more peace. You will also have more independence, since no one is covertly influencing your decisions. Your life will be much happier without manipulative people in your relationships.

Don't be a victim any longer. Read on to make your life happier and more wholesome with the right people. You don't need that negativity and control anymore, so learn how to do away with it for good.

Chapter 1: Identify If You Are The Victim Of Manipulation

Are You A Victim Of Manipulation?

No one likes being manipulated. It leaves a bad taste in your mouth when you realize that someone has toyed with your emotions or used your own nature to somehow use you. Manipulators will skillfully turn your very talents, strengths, and weaknesses into tools that they then use to their own advantages. You are just a tool, or a playing piece, and you have been moved around the manipulator's game board without giving your consent. Naturally, you are going to feel violated, betrayed, and even hurt. You are going to have trouble trusting the person who manipulated you and you are going to have trouble forgiving yourself.

Chances are, if you feel any of these things, then you are indeed a victim. The trouble with being a victim is that there is usually little you can do to change the outcome and beat the manipulator already. You may also have trouble pinpointing just why you feel so angry and used, since manipulators are great at evading detection and confrontation.

Trust your gut. If you feel you are being manipulated, then you are. There are no concrete rules on how to know when you are being manipulated, or how to prove it. You just have to trust yourself.

However, there are some signs that are relatively universal to the game of manipulation. Learning these can help you reaffirm your feelings and understand what has happened to you.

Someone Got You To Do Something You Didn't Want To

One of the major warning signs that you have been manipulated is that you did something you didn't feel right about or didn't want to do. When this happens, you know that someone influenced you. You may not even realize how and that doesn't truly matter. What matters is that you know someone is manipulative and now you can guard yourself against him or her in the future.

You Feel Guilty

Manipulators love to use guilt [1]. Guilt is the number one emotion they play on to get you to do things for them or to get you to forgive their obnoxious behavior. Thus, if you always feel bad for someone or always feel guilty in a relationship, then chances are you not doing anything wrong. The manipulator is just playing on your guilt to get things out of you.

A manipulator might do tons of nice things for you so that you feel as if you owe him one [2]. This plays on Cialdini's principle of reciprocity, where you make someone feel like they owe you for the nice favor you did them. A manipulator may constantly put you down and point out your mistakes so that you feel bad for what you do wrong. He may even constantly bring up and exaggerate things you have done wrong, to keep you held by chains of the past. Think of him as a puppeteer, using guilt and other emotions as strings to jerk you around.

Excessive guilt in any relationship is unhealthy. Forgive yourself. Then watch out for your partner's or friend's attempts to get you to feel guilty again. Don't let guilt influence your decisions, as that is exactly what the manipulator wants [6]. Also, don't feel guilty when someone does nice things for you that you didn't ask him or her to do. That's just a ploy for emotional blackmail.

Other signs of emotional blackmail include feeling ashamed of who you are or not good enough [2]. Manipulators prey on and cultivate these feelings to weaken you. You should never allow a person to make you feel low about yourself all of the time. Hearing a lot of insults and criticism can show that you are being made to feel ashamed and guilty [2]. Also watch out for phrases like, "No one else can put up with you the way I can" or "What you make me deal with is astounding!" This is the manipulator's clever way of making you feel guilty and also so bad about yourself that you assume you can never leave, or else no one else will ever want you.

Being afraid of the manipulator is also common. You may fear his sudden flashes of anger, which will switch to lighter moods at any time without warning. You may experience something called FOG, which is an acronym for fear, obligation, and guilt [2]. This is where a manipulator uses fear to scare you into obligation and guilt to keep you from confronting him.

Passive Aggressive Behavior

Many manipulators will refuse to speak their minds – and you'll find out why in the next chapter. They smile, agree, and say what you want to hear to keep you happy. Then they go do what they want. Or, they do what you want and throw a fit, pout, or deliberately do a bad job so that you feel bad for asking them a favor. Both behaviors are forms of passive aggression, which are common ways for the manipulator to get out of communicating.

If someone tells you what you want to hear and then does the opposite or acts put upon when doing you a favor that he agreed to do in the first place, you are being manipulated. Ignore this childish behavior and move on.

You Are Never Right

A manipulator will never break down and apologize or admit to guilt. He will instead make it seem like you are the one in the wrong. You will never be right in this relationship, and you will never win an argument.

A manipulator will use a variety of tactics to remain

right in all situations. He may lie compulsively, even when he knows you know the truth. He may make up ridiculous accusations to deflect the spotlight away from himself. He may deny everything, even if you have solid proof. And finally, he may just make you feel as if this is all your fault and you were wrong for even starting the argument in the first place. The only thing you can predict for certain is that he will not ever say sorry and admit to being wrong. It's always your fault and you are always wrong!

This behavior is most common with borderline personality disorder and narcissistic personality disorder sufferers. These people would rather die than admit to being wrong. It is a matter of ego to them, and their fragile egos are the centers of their universes.

Don't be surprised if a person denies everything – even things you are sure of! Gaslighting is a tactic where a manipulator makes you feel crazy by denying what you know to be true. An extreme example would be someone arguing that the sky is green when you know it's blue! They do this to evade responsibility while also disabling your trust in your perception.

Stick by your guns and know that you're right. Don't let the manipulator switch everything back onto you, lie, or gaslight you to get out of the truth. You'll learn more about how to defend yourself in these situations in later chapters.

You Feel Insane

Building on the topic of the last chapter, you can expect to feel like you're going crazy around certain manipulators. As they gaslight you, you start to wonder if you are going nuts or if you are heading into the early stages of dementia. You remember things like yesterday and the manipulator swears that you aren't remembering things right. You believe things but he's making you question their veracity. You hear him say something and then he denies it later on.

If you feel that you have to record conversations with a person, that's a really bad sign that you are dealing with a manipulator. These people will change the very words they say just to mess with you. Get out of there ASAP.

Receiving The Silent Treatment

The silent treatment can be normal if someone is upset and needs a few days to cool off. It may also happen if someone decides he or she is done and walks away from you for good. But a person who uses this often as a way to hurt you and make you cave to his or her will is an emotional manipulator. The silent treatment is unbearable and the manipulator knows this. He knows that you will eventually break down and do something or say sorry to get the unbearable treatment to end. The best course of action is to continue ignoring him or her, and use the silent treatment back.

Forgive Yourself

The key to getting past manipulation is to forgive yourself. You are a victim, even though the manipulator has craftily convinced you otherwise. You have done nothing wrong except for having the rotten luck of meeting a person who exploited you.

The first key to healing is to finally recognize that you don't deserve to be treated this way. The manipulator will have dozens of reasons why you do deserve it and what you have done wrong. That's just all part of the manipulation. No one deserves this. And you can't be held accountable for one of your mistakes forever. Let go of the guilt and stop hanging on.

Also let go of the shame. You are not a bad person. Start to remember your good qualities, which the manipulator has helped you forget. Do things you are good at to remember who you once were before being broken by a manipulator. This will help you realize that you are able to love again and other people can and will want you. The manipulator only broke down your self-esteem to keep you near.

Don't let fear, shame, and guilt keep you with a manipulator. Also don't let things like money keep you in a job or living situation where you are stuck with a manipulative person. There is no need to fear this person; if he is using manipulation, then he is not strong enough to actually do anything to you anyway. His threats are empty.

The more time you spend away from the manipulator, the stronger and happier you will become. It is ideal to sever these relationships, even if it scares you. In the end, you will be fine. Only with time on your own will you begin to heal and move on. Then you will just have to take care to never look back or let another one into your life. That is where the information in the next few chapters comes in – as you learn how to identify, weaken, and block manipulators.

Chapter 2: Why Manipulators Manipulate

The No Communication Skills Types

Most manipulators are not actually bad people. The media portrays manipulators are these terrible, cold people who are out to get you. While that is true of Dark Triad personality types, which you will read about in depth in this chapter, it is not true of most people who manipulate. The truth of that matter is, most manipulators are regular people like you or me. They only manipulate others because they have not learned healthier means of communication.

A large majority of manipulators were raised in households where they had no voice. They were never taught to simply state how they felt, or say what they want. They found that pouting, tantrums, or other manipulation tactics were the only way to get what they wanted. They also learned to never speak about their emotions to reach healthy resolutions, so they use alternative means.

These people are often from homes where they were criticized a lot and punished for speaking up against their parents. They may have grown up with a lot of siblings, so they had to compete for attention. Or they may just have had parents who were also manipulative, so that was the only model for communication they ever had.

How To Spot These Manipulators

Just because these manipulators don't have a horrible end game does not mean that their behavior is not harmful. Being able to spot them is a good way to start protecting yourself. These people generally don't have some huge, elaborate game plan, and they don't generally intend to hurt anyone. But you can tell they are manipulators because of their lack of directness.

The first sign is passive aggressive behavior. These types will not express their true anger in a healthy, constructive way. Instead, they smile, comply with what you want, and then act put out or burdened.

They may set up unpleasant consequences to make you feel bad for what you are having them do. They use this passive aggressive behavior to force you to conform to their emotional needs, which they have never told you.

Another sign is that these people are vague. They never tell you outright why they want something or what they have planned. But you always find out about an ulterior motive somehow. Nothing is ever as it seems with these people.

Being very busy and having lots of things going on and lots of people involved in every scheme is another warning sign. These people are trying to use as many people as they can to get some ulterior motive accomplished. They tend to get their wires crossed and fail to keep their stories straight. It can feel like existing in a whirlwind around them as they attempt to manage several different layers of plans toward an unseen, unclear goal.

Another sign is selfish, immature behavior, like throwing fits or pouting like a petulant child. This is another way these types will get you to do what they want without ever communicating properly.

Pathological lying or stories that don't add up give you a clue into a person's intentions, as well. These people can't ever be honest or direct. They intentionally withhold lots of information, hoping to benefit from what you don't know later on.

The Low Self-Esteem Types

Some people will manipulate out of low self-esteem. They use emotional manipulation to lower your self-esteem and hurt you without doing anything direct that you can call them on. Thus, they make themselves feel better as they deflate your balloons, so to speak.

An example may be Susan, who seems so sweet and

helpful at church. You meet her for lunch and feel really connected to her, as she confides little things in you. You end up spilling out your heart to her about your marriage troubles, thinking that she will understand and comfort you. Susan does both of these things and you leave lunch feeling great. The next Sunday at church, however, everyone is staring at you with sympathy and whispering about how your husband cheated on you. You confront Susan about divulging your personal business and she acts miffed at you and says that you are being a bad friend. "I was only helping everyone understand what you are going through. Honestly, I can't believe that you are mad at me! I've been such a good friend, haven't I?"

Daniel is your work buddy. You get lunch and play golf on weekends. One weekend, he asks you about your dating life and you casually mention that you are trying online dating. That Monday. as you stride into the office, everyone is making fun of you for the cheesy one-liners you put in your dating profile. When you confront Daniel for telling people, he tells you that you are just being sensitive and that you need a sense of humor to get through the brutality of adult dating.

Your mom is a wonderful person overall. But she is very good at making you feel bad about yourself without saying anything mean. She has always done this and you don't understand why or even how. You get your dream job and you call her to tell her the great news. She congratulates you and then says, "How are you going to get there?"

"Well, I'm going to move to the city. It'll cut my commute in half if I do that."

"But how will you afford it? I know you don't have much saved."

"I will, Mom, don't worry."

"And the city is so full of crime."

By the end of the conversation, you feel completely deflated. All of your joy in getting your dream job is replaced by anxiety and hopelessness. Your mom managed to rob your joy and rev up your anxiety in just five minutes. She is able to say that she is just worried about you, like any mother would be about her children, so you can't be mad at her. She will never admit that she did something wrong by tearing you down.

All of these vignettes are prime examples of people who manipulate you into feeling bad about yourself somehow. The first two are people who make you feel comfortable so that you tell them information, then they tell everyone else to humiliate you and strip away your sense of comfort and safety. They gain something from this – a balm for their own low self-esteem. By making everyone focus on your flaws and your imperfections, they manage to feel better about themselves and make themselves look better in comparison to you. Yet when you try to get mad at them, they are able to evade accountability with some sort of mind game. You will read that phrase, "evade accountability," a lot in this book because it's a classic manipulator behavior.

In the final example about a worried mother, she may very well be worried, but she used those worries to try to cancel your pride and joy. Why she does this is not clear – she maybe trying to manipulate you to stay nearer to her or she maybe trying to lower your self-esteem because she never got her own dream job in her lifetime. You will never know the reason because most manipulative people are great at hiding their true motives. All you know is that she has managed to play with your emotions and now you no longer look forward to working at your dream company. She is also able to evade accountability because she uses her maternal nature and the nature of your relationship with each other to prevent you from feeling rightfully angry at her.

How To Spot The Low Self-Esteem Type

The first key is to always be leery of a stranger who tries to become your best friend. These people may just be really nice – or they may be buttering you up to get information from you that they can later use. Avoid confiding in the people who make you feel like confiding the most until you really know them and have observed how they behave around other people.

Watch out for the busybody types. These are the warm, friendly people who talk to everyone and are always rushing off for some social engagement. These people are the ones who must know everything about everyone and collect people under their wings. Often this is so that they can have a network of victims to use and extort, or so that they can get information on people to spread around.

Manipulators like this are often charming. They will

try to trick you into giving the most information that you can. They want to know about your life, your interests, and your feelings toward every other person. The person who comes up to you and says, "Hey, what do you think of Claire?" is fishing for information that she can repeat back to Claire to make you look bad. The person who asks you about your marriage and expresses concern when she barely knows you is trying to feel better about her own marriage.

Gossips are often manipulators. They get information out of you and then either distort it or repeat it to everyone else. With this little game, they make you look bad to others. When a person gossips about other people to you, or tries to commiserate with you about how much you both hate the same person, beware. Any person who stands there talking badly about people who are not present will talk badly about you once you leave the room, too.

Also, watch out for those who appear to be in power. They acquired that power somehow, and I guarantee you it was through manipulating others to get their way. Often, people who possess very tiny bits of power, such as church potluck organizes, head nurses, or HOA or PTA presidents, are the most manipulative ones. They let their tiny bits of power go to their heads. These are the people who will do their best to lower your self-esteem in order to bolster their own egos and keep their power by smearing your reputation.

The friend who must always one-up you is a manipulator. If you broke your toe, he once almost had his leg amputated. If you are drunk, he can handle so much more liquor than you can. If you got a great job, his job has way better benefits and way more vacation time. The friends who turned everything into a silly competition are trying to prove that they are somehow better than you. They have low self-esteem and are trying to always beat you so that you can never appear to be the victor. You may not see a friendship as a power struggle or competition, but he or she does. This type of friend does not want to celebrate your victories or comfort your hardships; he or she just wants to be better than you to repair his or her eternal sense of inadequacy.

You may also see this in the person who must argue with your victories. Say you win a competition at work and proudly display your award plaque. All he has to say is, "You only won by one more sale than me." He is belittling your accomplishments to take away your sense of victory. Since he can't be the winner, he doesn't want you to feel like a winner either. These people will do anything to belittle you and take away your happiness. That way, they aren't alone in their misery.

Beware of the person who is always a victim. This person has the most rotten luck in history. Everything he does falls apart; everyone he knows betrays him. These chronic victims are usually manipulators who burn their bridges and twist things to make themselves look innocent. They will eventually manipulate you, too. They often have low self-esteem and little ability to take care of themselves. Thus, they must manipulate others to get ahead in life, and they get bitter when that strategy fails.

Watch out for the people who overtly criticize you, call you names, and otherwise bully you. These people are attempting to goad you to become defensive. Then you are trying to prove yourself to them, and you may even make a fool out of yourself. This gives them power that they feed off of. They will enjoy seeing you get angry or sad or defensive because it means they can provoke your emotions and cause you the same emotional discomfort or pain they feel all of the time. They will love it even more if you break down crying or start yelling in front of others, losing your composure and making yourself look weak and foolish to bystanders. If you start denigrating them or calling them names back, you stoop to their level and prove to everyone else that you are just as bad.

Finally, you may encounter lots of criticism in these low self-esteem manipulators. These people can find fault with perfection. They must put down and criticize every little thing. They do this to keep power over you. As long as you don't think too highly of yourself, you will never think that you are good enough to seek a better partner, friend, or colleague. This shows that they know they don't have much to offer you; they suffer from chronic low self-esteem, which they mask with meanness. The problem with their strategy is that you will soon tire of being put down, you will see their tactics for what they are, you will realize that you are not gaining anything from the relationship, and eventually, you will move on to greener pastures.

How To Handle Low Self-Esteem Types

The best approach to handling manipulators with low self-esteem is to ignore their pitiful and pathetic digs and their bait. As they criticize you or one-up you, ignore it. They are looking for a defensive response or a competitive one. They are trying to make you struggle to prove yourself. Then they feel in control. You can keep the control for yourself by offering a smile and no other response to their mean words.

If someone starts to call you names or say cruel things to get a rise out of you, just smile and say, "I believe that saying such things denotes a lack of communication skills and maturity. I don't have time for this. We can talk when you calm down and decide to use more polite language." Then walk away. The person will likely escalate and yell at you, but that makes him or her look bad, not you. You handled yourself with grace and aplomb; all anyone can do is commend you.

It is also wise to avoid divulging much information to anyone whom you don't know well. Let a person prove his trustworthiness before you share even the tiniest detail of your life. Certainly don't confide your troubles in people you don't know well, or people who gossip and talk badly about others. You can give vague answers to their fishing questions to show them that you are not an easy nut to crack. They will move on to easier targets and leave you alone very quickly.

Don't get caught in a gossip's triangle. Somehow gossips will cause trouble and then get out of any blame. They continue to play their games without consequences forever. The key is to just not play. When someone starts to gossip to you, say, "I don't like to talk about people when they're not here." That will shut the person down, since that is hardly a normal response. If a gossip tries to tell you what someone else said about you, don't take the bait to say anything defensive or speak ill of the person in subject; you are simply being triangulated by the gossip. Respond by saying, "I find it interesting that he/she felt comfortable telling that to you. What were you saying about me?" This will throw the gossip off so much and leave him or her shaken. It will teach him or her not to involve you in silly triangulation games because you are smarter than all of that.

Don't let charm blind you. The most charming people are often the most malignant. You can smile at them, laugh at their jokes, and even accept their dinner invitations, but don't count them as friends just yet. Take your time with these people until you see their true colors. More often than not, these people are very ugly on the inside. You will be able to tell when they denigrate servers or maids, start to gossip, or tell a lie. Just give them time to slip up.

When it comes to people in power, your best bet is to respect their power and stroke their egos at every chance. This will make them like you and cease seeing you as a threat. Then you will deal with fewer games. If you are indeed a threat, you can surprise the person by suddenly running for his office or position out of the blue. The surprise will throw him off.

The Controlling Types

Some people rise to power in a relationship or other setting by using a mixture of powerful manipulation techniques. These people don't know how to build a solid, loving relationship. They just want to control the relationship.

The first sign is using guilt trips, the silent treatment, or some sort of other punishment to impose their will on you. An example may be the mother who refuses to speak to her child for days on end because he didn't like the outfit she bought him; he finally breaks down and apologizes. Another might be the wife who withholds sex from her husband and acts coldly toward him until he breaks down and apologizes for a very minor transgression. People who punish you until you do what they want are the ones who are manipulating you for control.

These people often use a negative reinforcement strategy to impose their will on others. But sometimes they mix in positive reinforcement. They offer rewards for you fulfilling their wishes. While there is nothing wrong with offering someone a reward for doing what you want, it is very harmful when mixed with other strategies. It creates a confusing and emotionally scarring game.

How To Deal With Controlling Types

Indifference is the best strategy when dealing with these types. They extort you emotionally to get what they want. Not playing the game and giving them the reaction they desire will cause you to win. It will also drive the manipulator away in search of a more malleable target.

When someone gives you the silent treatment, just ignore them too. They will eventually break down and even shout at you for ignoring them. Just continue to ignore them. They want you to beg and plead for them to speak to you again, so don't give in.

Also don't accept their rewards or take their threats seriously. They are just mixing strategies in a desperate attempt to get you to comply. Not giving in involves ignoring or even laughing at what they are laying on the table. They won't know how to deal with this and they may break down in front of others, proving what psychotic individuals they can be.

The Co-Dependent Types

Co-dependent people are seldom bad people. But their need to be supported by others makes them do bad things. These people tend to dislike themselves and have trouble being alone. Thus, they will enter any kind of relationship they can find just to have someone around. You will often see them enter bad relationships and then fight to stay in them, never leaving until they have absolutely no other choice. They may also repeat bad patterns, such as serial monogamy or one abusive relationship after another.

Many people who stay in abusive relationships are co-dependent types who would rather tolerate abuse than be alone. While abuse is never right, these people tend to perpetuate said abuse because they never make the choice to leave. They are getting some benefit out of staying, which is why they choose to do so.

These people are so afraid to be alone, or so unable to be alone, that they will do anything to keep their partner or friend around. They often will resort to emotional manipulation to accomplish this. An example might be the boyfriend who threatens suicide every time you say you are going to leave, or the girlfriend who says you are a terrible person and you are lucky to have her because no one else would put up with your nonsense. Using threats, emotional blackmail, or criticism, they make you feel as if you can't ever exit the relationship. If you do, something bad will happen to you or to the manipulator.

How To Spot These Types

The first big red flag that someone is co-dependent is when they want to move too fast in a relationship. Be it a romantic partner who wants to move in after a month of dating, or a friend who wants to make you her maid of honor after knowing you just a week, these people force relationships to happen at an unsafe rate. They may use a lot of charm and guilt to pressure you to move too fast with them.

The next big red flag is a spotty or bad history of relationships. The person may have an endless string of exes who abused her, or a long series of bad friends who stabbed him in the back. This person is never accountable for how these relationships fell apart. He or she is always the victim. Yet he or she cannot explain why he or she put up with such poor treatment from an ex or past friend for so long. Often, people tend to abandon this person because they just can't keep up with his or her constant needs and clingy behavior, causing this person to have few friends.

The final big red flag would be that this person is indecisive and cannot make decisions or do things alone. Eating alone seems like this person's worst nightmare. This person can't do anything in life without the emotional support and approval of another. This person may not even work, seeking others to pay his or her bills. You get a sense of desperation and neediness from day one, be it physical, emotional, financial, or otherwise. Almost immediately, this person will start asking you for more and more time, financial help, or approval for every little decision.

How To Handle Co-Dependent Types

The best strategy in handling a co-dependent person is to avoid the relationship altogether. You may like this person or even love this person, but co-dependency is never healthy. This person must learn to live alone and to like him- or herself before he or she can enter a healthy relationship. Otherwise, he or she will make various mistakes out of a desperate need for your support. He or she will also most likely turn to dire measures and manipulation to keep you around. You will never be safe in a relationship with a co-dependent person.

If you absolutely must be in a relationship of some kind with this person, then you need to set boundaries from day one. Make it clear that you need time and space of your own. Make one night a week without this person sacred. When this person asks for all of your time, say that you can spend Saturday with him or her. If this person needs your validation for every opinion and decision, just say, "I think you have sound judgment. What do you think?" When this person needs money, encourage him or her to earn it somehow and point them in the direction of jobs, side gigs, or other means to earn the funds. Encourage this person to respect your healthy perspective on life and relationships to train him or her to be the same.

Also, never move too fast in a relationship. Always wait until you are ready. Moving in, buying a house together, having a baby – these are big life decisions. You must think about them carefully and logically. Don't let a person use charm, guilt, or some other manipulation tactic to coerce you into something you do not feel ready for. If a person cannot respect your need for time to make a decision, it may be wise to part ways.

It is a good idea to always use some measure of birth control that you can control yourself when entering a sexual relationship with such a person. These are the types who may tamper with birth control or lie about taking birth control in order to get pregnant and thus trap you in the relationship before you are even sure you want to be with him or her. Men may poke holes in condoms or lie about wearing them, so always supply your own when having sex with a co-dependent man. Women may lie about taking birth control pills so always use a condom with such a woman.

Vindictive Types

Almost all manipulators will turn into vindictive types when they are not getting their way. But some people only whip out the manipulative games when they can't see any other way to get what they want. Vindictive types become ruthless and even dangerous.

A good example would be the mother who refuses to let the father see his kids as vindication for him dating someone new. Another example would be the boss who gives you a terrible reference out of anger that you left his company, even though you left on good terms and performed well at your role there. Yet another would be the neighbor who plays loud music late into the night to get revenge for the louder-than-usual get-together you had last week to celebrate your army spouse's return home from Afghanistan. These people do little things to hurt you and bother you, instead of confronting you in a healthy way and being honest about their feelings. Often, their revenge tactics are quite effective because they hit you where it counts.

The worst vindictive types are those who know you well. Exes, old friends, old bosses, and family members are the ones who can make the most powerful enemies.

How To Handle Vindictive Types

Often, you can beat a vindictive person at his or her own game just by apologizing. Even if you don't feel that an apology is owed, you should still do it for future peace. It is ideal to walk up to the person and use empathy, saying, "I understand how you must feel. I'm sorry you feel that way. I probably would feel that way in your position."

Avoid using "you" terms, like "You are doing this" or "You need to stop." These terms sound accusatory.

They will trigger the person's defenses to go up and then the ensuing discussion will be useless.

It is far better to use "I" terms. These terms show your perspective and convey empathy. "I don't like how you play music late into the night. It does not seem fair to me. I'm sorry for the loud party last weekend and I promise it won't happen again."

Once you do this, you can start repairing the relationship or appeasing the vindictive manipulator's emotions. The manipulator most likely won't even try to evade accountability if you take this approach. His or her need to get revenge will also go away, as he or she realizes you are just a person who is prone to mistakes too. Acknowledging a hurt person's emotions can be the salve that helps those wounds heal and removes all need for revenge. Even if you don't agree with the person's emotions, they are not yours to disagree with. It is far better to accept them and acknowledge them to make your life much easier. Don't look at this as giving into what the manipulator wants, because the manipulator just wants revenge rather than an apology. Instead, view it as a way to help yourself avoid further harm.

Imagine how this might help in the case of a vindictive mother withholding kids from their dad. The most common approach the father will take is calling her selfish and yelling at her for hurting the children. While the father's anger is certainly justified and her actions are obviously wrong, yelling at her will only make her angrier. A father in this situation would be much wiser to tell her, "I'm sorry you are hurt over our relationship. I hope that I can make things right in time. For now, I think it's best for the kids that I am in their lives. If you have misgivings about my new partner, you can get to know her, so that you can decide if you want the kids around her." This mature and gentle approach may not be what she deserves, but it is what she is least expecting. She will be promptly disarmed and more amicable thereafter. The same type of thing can be done for the vindictive neighbor or boss.

The Dark Triad Types

The Dark Triad refers to a group of personality disorders that cause people to view others as pawns or tools, not real human beings with real feelings. These people are cold, ruthless, and toxic because they have no ability to feel remorse or empathy. Life is a long, drawn-out game to them that they eagerly play. It is best to avoid these types, but you might end up working for or with one, or you might have one in your family. Thus it is imperative to learn their traits and how to guard yourself from their wicked head games.

The Dark Triad contains psychopaths, Machiavellians, and narcissists [4]. These three types of people are particularly malevolent in their behavior and traits. Most criminals, such as repeat offenders, sex offenders, and serial killers, score highly on the Dark Triad traits.

Machiavellianism refers to people who plot to undermine and deceive others for their own gain. They are manipulators by default. They have no sense of right or wrong, and don't care about others. Everyone is here to serve their own needs. Often these people can be seen in authority positions, where they manipulator and exploit others for power and wealth.

Narcissists, or people with narcissistic personality disorder, are not always harmful people. Malignant narcissists, however, are. The narcissist is grandiose, egocentric, and self-centered. He must be the center of the universe and he must be lavished with praise and attention at all times. He will manipulate others to worship him and he may get a sick joy from putting others down or hurting others in order to prove how great he is. Making people cry can make him feel like he won somehow; making people act out in rage will prove to him that he is divine because he can control his temper; and proving that he's right at all times without ever apologizing for anything is key to his ego-centered happiness. He will use people to give him attention, called using people as his "narcissistic supply."

Psychopathy, or antisocial personality disorder, refers to people who feel no empathy or remorse. They often don't feel anything at all. They are cold and practical and calculating, treating life like a game and using people to reach their goals. They may harm others to get dominance and control in some way. Most serial killers are psychopaths, but not all psychopaths are serial killers. You will see psychopaths in positions of power, ranging from church clergy to the government to the police force. They can be great friends because they are loyal to those who serve their needs and they can be great at their jobs because they are laser-focused and goal-oriented, using logic instead of emotion. But they can also be incredibly harmful because they don't consider humans from emotional standpoints and don't experience empathy.

Another personality disorder that does not appear in the Dark Triad but can be considered just as harmful is borderline personality disorder. Borderlines are not harmful people by default; in fact, they may even mean well. But they are so scared of abandonment and so sensitive to criticism that they will manipulate others for control, co-dependency, and even emotional gratification. They will refuse to be wrong just like narcissists because it affronts their delicate egos. They will hurt other people and manipulate people to remain in control, since they greatly fear losing control.

How To Handle Dark Triad Types

Dark Triad types are both dangerous and difficult to deal with. Thus, you must take great care in handling them. By far the best option is avoidance. If you can, stay away from these people. Try to identify their scary traits through their charm. Getting to know someone will soon reveal if they are a Dark Triad personality type.

However, it is not always possible to avoid these people. You may encounter them a lot at work, for instance, or have one in your family. In this case, it is best to just stroke their egos. Do what they ask, smile, and tell them what good people they are. This inspires them to be more loyal to you.

This does not mean that you have to be a pawn. You can tell them no if you want to. Just be prepared for a battery of harassment or further manipulation. Always have your guard up around these people because things are never what they seem.

Also avoid sharing personal information with these people. They are good at making you feel comfortable and confiding in them. Later, they use what you told them to hurt you. Remember, they have no remorse or empathy. Therefore, keep your mouth shut and only mention what they need to know. You can even politely refuse to answer personal questions or evade these questions with polite replies and then a subject change.

Finally, keep an eye on things that are vulnerable, such as your children, your bank account, or your job security. Make sure this person isn't somehow tampering with your life. You want to keep good records to prove your innocence should one of these types start to use your most precious resources against you. Don't trust them with keys, sensitive information, or access to your personal life.

Chapter 3: Beating The Vicious Cycle Of Manipulation

Manipulation is a vicious cycle. Why? Because once a person is able to manipulate you, they create a complex web of guilt, fear, or reciprocity around you that you feel unable to escape. They are able to get more and more out of you, until they leech you dry. Then they are likely to get angry with you or even abandon you for more willing victims once you have nothing left to provide them.

The vicious cycle of manipulation is hard to escape solely because humans tend to make decisions based on emotion [6]. Manipulators exploit this fact quite talentedly. They make sure that you never feel able to tell them no and continue to make the decisions they want based on the emotions they lead you to feel. Learning to use logic when making decisions and learning to identify manipulation while it is happening can help you recognize this trap and then pull yourself out of it, unscathed.

Use Logic Instead Of Emotion When Making A Decision

You don't want to do something for someone, but you feel obligated to because of guilt. This is a sign that you are being manipulated. Take a step back and reason through why you don't want to do something and how you can gain by not doing it. Use a mental cost-benefit analysis to remove the sense of obligation and make a decision based on plain facts.

This cost-benefit analysis is simple. Just divide a piece of paper into two halves. One half is the costs, or cons, and the other half is the benefits, or pros. Weigh both sides of the decision with careful research and consideration until you can reach one that sits well with you. Do this without asking the manipulator so that you can maintain a clear head.

It has been found in a study that people tend to use logic poorly when they are in negative moods, and better logic in positive moods [7]. Thus, you may want to improve your mood by doing something that makes you happy, putting on some light music, or even just relaxing in the sunshine or a bubble bath for a while before tackling a big decision. It will improve your logical ability.

Sometimes, you need to make a decision based on emotion, not logic. An example might be when you are deciding to pursue a romantic relationship with somebody or get to know a new friend. In this case, your gut will do you more good than any cost-benefit analysis. Manipulators tend to use charm to cloud your emotions and disarm you, making you feel smitten long before you should. Be wary of people who are too charming or too perfect and take your time. Always listen to that sense that something isn't right; this is not paranoia, no matter what you may try to convince yourself.

It is wise to listen to your friends and closest loved ones on these issues. If you have been blinded by a manipulator, you may think that other people are just jealous or being overprotective. As they urge you to take a harder look at this guy or gal, you argue, "This person is perfect! Can't you be happy for me for once? This isn't like last time!" But maybe you should consider what they have to say and take a step back. Your loved ones can see things from a different perspective and they may be able to spot bad signs that you have been blinded to by the manipulator. You are not a dumb or naïve person, but as the victim of manipulation, your perception cannot always be trusted. Using outside perspective and letting your loved ones get to know a person as you get to know him or her can really help you avoid some heartache down the road.

Be very wary of people who don't want to meet your friends or family. They may claim that they are just shy and nervous, but a normal person with nothing to hide will work to overcome that and try to meet your circle. The same can be said for a co-worker, friend, or client who seems to only want to talk to you. Get them to talk to other people you know to gauge how they really are with their people skills.

Be even more wary of those who push you and rush

you into something too fast. This could be a boyfriend who wants to move in right away or a client who wants to work with you without any formal interviewing and negotiating. It can be a salesman who goads you to buy something because it's soon to run out. Don't let urgency or your own desires for romance or success make you neglect caution and common sense. Manipulators play on what you want and will make you a deal that you feel is foolish to turn down, so you need to look past your deepest wants and instead consider the reality of the proposition you are facing.

Just Say No

The above is more about avoiding manipulation and halting it before it begins. But let's see you're already caught in the cycle. If you know or suspect someone is manipulating you, just say no to everything they ask from then on. This shows them that you are no longer a tool for their use. They may react in a number of unpleasant ways, all of which you will read about and learn to address properly in a later chapter. For now, though, just worry about saying no.

Saying no is surprisingly difficult with manipulators because they are proficient at eroding your boundaries and sometimes even canceling your sense of self-worth. Using emotional games, they are able to make you feel that you have to say yes. They even condition you to feel bad for saying no and good for saying yes in many cases, as well. Thus, saying no is not as easy or as simple as it sounds.

You may encounter a manipulator who uses the foot in the door, where he asks a small favor and then asks more. He may use consistency and commitment, where he gets you to commit to something so you keep committing to more and more [2]. He may do you favors and then use reciprocity to get favors out of you [2]. Or he may simply use guilt and emotional blackmail to make you feel as if you have to do something [3]. All of these games can make saying no hard.

That doesn't mean you can't do it. The best strategy to make saying no possible is to focus on what the manipulator has done to you. Let yourself be angry and don't let his games carry any weight. Think about how you have been wronged and violated and used. Your ego should be bruised from this; let that pain fill you so that you don't feel obligated to somehow help this person.

Another key is to avoid the manipulator. Don't let him sweet talk you into changing your mind. Don't let him turn on the charm, or the threats, or the guilt. Also don't let him make any sales pitches that make things appear like good ideas or awesome deals. The more you limit contact, the less of a hold the manipulator has on your emotions. Then you are better equipped to shut down the manipulation and say no.

When someone manipulates you with a reward or even sex, you may have trouble looking past that. This is where logic comes into play. Think about the true cost of that reward, or that sex. Is it worth what this person plans to put you through, or already has put you through? Will you really benefit that much in the end by giving him or her what he or she wants? The answer is most likely no. But you must use rational logic to see that, instead of emotion. Taking a step back is essential.

Ask For Clear Terms And More Time

Manipulators will use vague language to confuse you or escape accountability later on if they don't deliver what you expected. By leaving conversations open-ended, they lead you to make an expectation that is not the same as what they plan to do. They will also rush you, so you don't have time to make a good decision and do your research. In both methods, they take away your ability to make an informed decision and coerce you into the one that benefits them.

You have to beat them at this game by demanding more time or more information. Demand clear terms. Demand that you go home and think about this. Demand that they stop talking and just let you make the decision. As they attempt to use the principle of scarcity to pressure you, just stay firm in your resolve [2]. You may hear things like, "This won't last" or "You'll be sorry for letting this deal go!" You will be sorrier if you don't let the deal go and chances are, the deal will still be waiting the next day after you take some time to think.

Information overload is one way that manipulators keep you from making a decision. As they spew facts and authority endorsements and statistics, your eyes cross and you stop paying attention. That's when they sneak in ominous details, lie about terms, or omit important facts. They may speak so much or so fast that you can't keep up, so that you don't pay attention to important details. Salespeople are the worst at this, but any manipulator who is trying to get you to make a decision will do these things. In these cases, just ask him to speak more slowly and clearly and have him repeat everything. Ask for everything in writing and read it over carefully. Manipulators who are out to con you won't like this – and that's a sign to back out of this deal ASAP!

Leaving A Manipulator

When you figure out that someone is a manipulator, you realize that the relationship is toxic and you need to get out. But you are often held by a web of emotional entanglement that is hardly easy to escape. The manipulator may have convinced that you owe him or her and that no one else could love you. You may even be scared of threats that the manipulator has held over your head.

Start to ask questions to prove what is really going on. For example, one woman's narcissistic husband loved to tell her that everyone hated her and she believed him. One day, however, she had enough. She asked him, "Who hates me?"

"Well...the neighbors do!"

"I happen to be close to all the neighbors, Tom." Then, right there, she began to recognize the toxic web he had spun around her to keep her as his mental captive. Just seeing the truth helped her start to heal and get out. Eventually, she left him.

Susan Forward discusses how manipulators blind you with FOG, fear, obligation, and guilt. The first part is to address the fear. What do you really have to fear? What do you have to lose? Will the manipulator's threats truly ruin your life? Maybe reevaluate your priorities and investigate if their threats are empty. As the case with the example above, her husband used the threat that everybody hated her to make her fear leaving him and being alone. She started to question that because she knew in her heart it wasn't true and she learned his threat was empty. Many of these threats don't mean anything or they won't hurt you as much as the manipulator would have you believe.

The next step is questioning if you are truly obligated to this person. Are you happy? If not, you have no obligations left. You are not obligated to a lover, even if he or she has done some really nice things for you, because life is not all about equal give and take. You are not obligated to your boss to do more than your job and you are not obligated to take care of family members or friends just because they are in your life. Evaluate what the people in your life mean to you and if they milk things they have done for you to get a sense of obligation out of you. You may even consider what you have done for them or sacrificed for them to see that they really have not done as much for you as they would have you believe.

Lastly, address the guilt. Manipulators love to play with guilt, the worst human emotion [8]. In a study, people were willing to administer electric shocks to themselves for perceived guilt [8]. Manipulators will string you along forever with guilt. Look at what you have done and evaluate if it was truly bad to keep punishing yourself for. Evaluate if you have apologized and done anything to atone for it. If you have, then it's time to stop feeling guilty and stop letting the manipulator play you like a fiddle with that guilt.

Working through fog can be tough. You may need an outside perspective, like a friend or even a counselor, to realize the number that has been done to you. An outside perspective can help you gain clarity from the manipulator's web of lies and emotional manipulation. Don't be afraid to ask for help. Definitely don't expect help from the manipulator!

When you walk through the fog, you are able to leave. You realize that you have nothing to fear, no obligation to stay, and nothing to atone for. Now you can leave and begin the lengthy healing process.

Healing From Mental And Emotional Abuse

Once you have been through a manipulator's abuse, you are changed in many ways. The voice in your head changes, leading you to think of yourself in a more negative way and causing you to make decisions you normally wouldn't. The impact of this abuse can last long after you have told the manipulator in your life good-bye for good.

One of the first things manipulators do to abuse you is break down your sense of self-worth. They make you feel as if you are wrong for having healthy boundaries, just so that you let them violate you. They make you feel as if you look at the world wrong and you have something profoundly wrong with you. They do this by telling you that you are selfish when you want something, and saying that you can't take a joke when you get offended over something awful they say. With criticism repeated over a long enough period of time, they can make you believe whatever they said about you, eradicating your self-esteem and making you feel worthless.

Using gaslighting and other such tactics, they may also have made you doubt your sanity. Now you can't trust your instincts and feel totally out of it. Another thing this abuser may have done is smear your reputation and isolate you from friends and family, so you feel very alone with all of your bridges burned. By the end of the relationship, you feel like a wisp of who you once were and you don't know yourself anymore at all. You feel as if you have nothing left.

The first step is to start reaching out to old friends and family. Try to mend the bridges that your toxic relationship has burned. They may forgive you and reaffirm how much they love you. This will do wonders for your self-esteem. Don't try to address the smear campaign this person has done; just try to show all of those people that you are better than what the manipulator painted you as. It can take some time and work to repair all of the relationships damaged by the manipulator in your life once he or she has fully infiltrated it at every level.

Another good step is to join a support group, either online or in person. This helps you realize that you are not alone and what you are going through is normal. With that information, you can start to regain your sense of sanity. Counseling can also help you with this.

Find something you enjoy to help you make new connections and distract yourself from the pain. Stay busy with work, school, family, or whatever you have going on. These things can help you heal and find yourself again.

When you hear your manipulator's voice in your head, which is not uncommon, just think in a different voice. Start to use positive self-talk [9]. Positive self-talk helps you gain a more positive mood and higher self-esteem, which can certainly help in the depression and anxiety following an emotionally abusive relationship [9]. Try cheering yourself on from the third person for a while to grow your self-esteem, an endeavor that has proved successful in a study [9].

Finally, be gentle on yourself. Healing is not linear and you may have bad days after many good days. You have not backslid, you have just encountered a new challenge in the healing process. View each day as a new chance to do better. Always view your experience as a learning experience that you can grow from instead of feeling sorry for yourself. Accept that at times you may miss the abuser or even wish that you could get back together, but resist the urge to act on those feelings. They are normal and will pass in time. Going back will only hurt you more than before as the manipulator will be even worse to gain more control over you now that you have left.

Don't ever believe that you deserved what happened to you. You are a victim. You can learn from it and move on, but you never deserved any of it. Keep your head up and take it day by day.

Chapter 4: How To Confront A Manipulator

I like to think of manipulators as slippery fish. When you try to catch them in their acts, they find a clever way to evade the truth and wriggle out of your grasp. Most of them are adept at turning things around on you to make you feel at fault. Others just slip out of any accusation and completely escape taking accountability, every time, without fail.

Confrontation with manipulators is a strange and delicate art. If you are not careful and equally clever, you will find yourself sorry for confronting a manipulator as he switches tactics, throws things back in your face, or starts to escalate into serious violence or psychological warfare. Prevent this by learning to handle manipulators well, based on type.

Don't Take On Battles You Can't Win

It's time to be mature and admit that you are not as

skilled as some manipulators. Their games are too much to deal with. If you confront them, they will get the best of you and drive you to act in a way that you didn't want. You might lose your temper, start crying, or end up apologizing if these are your tendencies. None of these things help.

Therefore, accept your skill level. You may just need to walk away and give up on confrontation. Perhaps you should send an email so you have a layer of digital protection. You can also have someone else mediate.

Don't Be Accusational Or Emotional

When confronted, manipulators are often cool. They may act offended or they may play it off. They certainly won't admit to any wrongdoing. You would be wise to do the same thing. Take the high road with a smile, polite language, and serenity. Don't ever raise your voice or get emotional. All of these things give the manipulator what he or she wants.

You can gain dominance using power posing [10]. It is crucial to appear taller than your opponent to assert yourself. Hold firm eye contact and speak firmly. Don't fidget or break eye contact, as that shows weakness. Keeps your spine ramrod straight, your shoulders back, and your head held high. When sitting, don't cross your legs or arms and take up as much space as you can. The key here is to make yourself look powerful. This will intimidate your manipulator friend.

You can try to use insincere flattery, and start the confrontation with a compliment [11]. All people respond well to this and love having their egos stroked [11]. Start the conversation with something akin to: "You are a great boss. I just need one thing from you." Or try, "I think you're a great person. I just wanted to talk about something."

Try using some easier and softer language. Don't use accusatory tones, like "You did this!" This just sets off the manipulator's defense mechanisms. Rather, use "I" messages like, "I felt this way when you did that." Be direct but use softer terms, like "take" instead of "steal." Passive language is better than active language. "This was done" rather than "You did this" sets people at ease more. These communication hacks help people feel better and less defensive, which makes the confrontation go more smoothly.

You can also turn the manipulation around on the manipulator. Try to point out how he will benefit and what he will gain from not manipulating you anymore. By focusing on his benefits rather than yourself, you will make more sense to him. A lot of manipulators lack empathy, so try avoiding keeping it focused on your feelings. That won't matter as much as convincing him what he will gain by respecting you. Offer him a reward of some kind if you can.

Stay On Topic

Manipulators will attempt to deflect and change the subject. This is how they avoid accountability. The key here is to stay on topic and don't let the manipulator change the subject.

Manipulators are great at suddenly bringing up something you did to get the attention off of themselves. Just say, "We're not talking about me." They may change the subject, so persist. They may start crying or threatening to hurt themselves to make you feel bad for even confronting them, so let them know that you aren't playing that game. If someone threatens suicide to get out of a confrontation, just stop playing the game and call the cops instead. That will shut that emotional blackmail down very quickly.

Present Evidence If You Can

Manipulators will attempt to deny everything or even

gaslight you about the truth. Having hard evidence to present is your best bet here. You want to have the texts, photos, bank statements, or whatever you need. Then, even if he lies, you can still know the truth for yourself. Some people will lie even in the face of obvious evidence, so don't expect this to cause him to break down and confess the truth. At least you can see through his lies and know him for who he really is now, though.

Accept That You May Not Win

It is a sad truth that most confrontations with manipulators will not go over well. You likely won't make any progress. The manipulator would rather die than admit to being wrong. Therefore, you may have to accept the fact that your confrontation will not yield the results you were hoping for.

It is still important to confront a manipulator. It keeps you from feeling guilty for never standing up for yourself. It also lets the manipulator know that he has overplayed his hand and you are aware of his behavior, so he may be more cautious and avoid manipulating you from now on.

A confrontation may also drive you to the point where you finally feel ready to cut the ties with the manipulator. It can be difficult to do this, especially with someone you feel close to. But confrontation will open your eyes to how infuriating manipulators are. Then you can feel better about breaking free and ending the relationship.

Understand that you may not make the manipulator want to change or fix anything. This is how the manipulator is – he won't change. Also understand that you can't set the past right. Use this knowledge to let go of the past and move forward, either with or without the manipulator in your life. Things will never change with this person, that's for certain. But they can change for you!

What To Do When A Manipulator Escalates

The tactics outlined in the last chapter are great ones and they work. But they fail to mention what happens when a manipulator escalates. Manipulators are hell-bent on getting what they want and they hate being confronted. When you confront one, you will encounter three different reactions:

1. The manipulator realizes that you are not an easy target so he backs off. This is common when a manipulator has just met you and has not had a chance to manipulate you before. It may also happen with people who are actually harmless and don't mean to do anything bad to you. But it is probably the least likely scenario.

2. The manipulator will switch tactics. Most of these people have a vast toolbox of manipulation methods that they use at any given time. Should one fail to work, they will whip out another one. The most common one they will use when confronted is

making you feel guilty for even thinking such a thing. Or they may try to make you feel as if you deserved what they did to you. They will do anything to twist the game back onto you and make it seem like your fault, and they are quite convincing. Be prepared for accusations, lies, and crocodile tears. Don't believe any of it. They may also simply try a new way to get you to do what they want, so continue to be resistant. This scenario is very likely to happen – almost guaranteed!

3.   The manipulator will become irrationally angry that you confronted him or her and will begin to escalate in rage. He or she can become downright scary. Now you are on his or her shit list and you can expect psychological warfare and all sorts of nefarious jabs at you. Your well-being is now jeopardized. This is most common from those who are in positions of power or who suffer from antisocial personality disorder or even narcissistic personality disorder. The best strategy to deal with this one is covered below.

Most manipulators want the path of least resistance. You will find that just saying no and standing up for yourself works great with these people. But when a manipulator escalates, you will find that his tactics are quite different. He will stop at nothing. He can become psychotic and violent, even. Once a manipulator escalates, the game changes. You now must tread very carefully.

The first rule of the new game is to avoid being scared of the manipulator. Have a mentality that you have nothing to lose and keep a power pose. This may make the manipulator leave you alone, since it's your fear that he or she is preying on. He or she hopes that you will relent to protect yourself. Don't do this. Don't let him or her win.

The second rule is to stay in your home court. Avoid meeting the manipulator somewhere outside of your comfort zone or being alone with him or her. If you leave the comfort of your familiar surroundings, you are more vulnerable. The manipulator knows this and will use it to scare you even more.

Resist the urge to get defensive or speak up for yourself. It is far better to keep your calm and stay rational. The manipulator who escalates is irrational and thus more comfortable with irrational behavior. If you blow your lid, it won't faze the manipulator at all. The best thing to do is to stay calm and keep your voice level. Don't attempt to diffuse the situation or defend yourself, just smile and nod. This will diffuse the situation far more than anything you could say.

To make this easier on yourself, repeat the mantra in your head: *I need to be better than this person.* Also think how this person must truly be miserable and let sympathy replace passion and anger. Remember that this person is irrational and can't be rationed with, and let that be a reminder to always be sympathetic and avoidant rather than defensive or critical.

Make sure you have lots of witnesses, as well. You don't want to be alone with this person. By always having people around you, the manipulator is less likely to do something truly dangerous or crazy. If you can't have witnesses, record the conversation secretly. That way, you have proof of what this person is doing if you need it. This could come in handy if you encounter this at work and must visit HR with a recording of your boss or co-worker threatening you.

When the person starts to cool down, you are able to ask with genuine curiosity, "What was that about?" This allows for discussion to begin. The manipulator realizes that exploding at you won't get you to back off, and he just made a fool of himself if others are around. Therefore, he is forced to talk. Or he may storm away in anger. Either way, he is off your back now!

Chapter 5: How To Weaken A Manipulator

Manipulators are empowered by two things: Their discretion and slippery inability to get caught on solid evidence, and their ability to make people do what they want. Taking these two things away from them will effectively weaken them and end their power streak. You really don't have to do anything else.

Keep Repeating The Question

The first step to weakening a manipulator is ensuring that the manipulator cannot evade accountability. One way a lot of manipulators do this is by bringing up irrelevant things to distract you, making you feel guilty, or simply changing the subject altogether.

You can counter this by repeating the question you are confronting him with. When he tries to change the subject, repeat the question. When he brings you up, say, "This isn't about me" and repeat the question.

When he attempts to distract you with a separate issue or fight or something you did, refuse to take his bait and repeat the question.

Being dogged will either break him down or else make him irate. Either way, he loses. You win. Consider irrational anger a sign that he is indeed guilty.

Show Him Hard Evidence

Getting some sort of hard evidence is a great way to corner a manipulator. Hard proof that he or she cheated, stole money, or otherwise did something wrong is great. You may also find hard evidence that he or she gaslighted you helpful as well.

Don't be surprised if this backfires, however. The manipulator may panic and deny everything, make up an outrageous lie or excuse, or continue to gaslight you. He or she may also confess and give you an empty apology. Basically, he or she will switch tactics. Just use the evidence to convince yourself and see through his or her games. Don't expect it to fix your relationship or force him or her to say sorry and actually mean it.

Walk Away

The manipulator wants to win and have control. By walking away and ending the relationship, you take that away from him or her. Thus you win and he or she is disabled. The toxicity can also finally end.

Don't tell him or her why. Just quit taking calls and visits and avoid him or her. Don't show up to his or her parties, dinners, or other events. Radio silence is vital to severing this Medusa's head.

See The Game For What It Is

The second factor – one that you will find most

effective – is refusing to give the manipulator what he or she wants. Be it an emotional breakdown, angry outburst, or apology, you know what this person wants. Don't do it under any circumstances.

By not giving him or her what is wanted, you take the power back. You fail to let this person trample all over you.

Figure out what he or she wants based on your gut reaction. If you want to react in anger, that's probably what he or she wants. Also look into the past. What have you done in the past in reaction? What has blown up in your face? That's a good clue into what the manipulator wants now.

Chapter 6: Specific Considerations For Manipulation In The Working Environment

The workplace may be the biggest hotbed of corruption and manipulation that you will encounter in your life. Manipulation is used to sell products and services, gain dominance in the workplace, and move up the corporate ladder. Most people in positions of power and skilled salespeople are talented manipulators, which is how they got their jobs. Lawyers, cops, and other professions are also professional manipulators and you will be manipulated if you work with them.

The Power Struggle

The most common type of manipulation you will encounter in the workplace involves intimidation for dominance. People want to get ahead, so they will manipulate you to scare you.

This manipulation is often subtle. Do you notice how

certain people make you feel intimidated and you don't know why? Your boss may appear to be a friendly guy, but his imposing presence always gives you some nerves, for instance.

This is partly because people will use their authority on you [2]. Authority is one of the principles of persuasion purposed by Robert Cialdini, a genius researcher into human persuasion and influence. An authority figure, such as a cop, boss, or lawyer, knows that he is an authority and uses his position to intimidate others. People with less power may pretend to be authorities or may get the support of authorities in order to be intimidating as well.

But it can be even more subtle than that. A person who intimidates you is often very aware of what he is doing. He is using subliminal signs to prove that he is someone to be reckoned with. He will appear taller with his posture, and bigger as well by spreading out his limbs when he walks or sits [10]. He will sit in a higher chair than you, or tower over you at your desk.

He will make hard eye contact and use firm handshakes. All of these little power moves work on the human subconscious to make you respect this person by recognizing that he is a leader of some kind.

He may also use cruel jokes to criticize you, or he may call you name and threaten you. All of this is meant to intimidate and denigrate you. If you get angry, you are called unprofessional. If you get insulted, you are told to lighten up and laugh a little. The truth is that you don't have to do any of that. Don't tolerate this. Say, "I don't find that funny" and walk away. Say, "I don't care for being called names. Let's talk when you can speak to me like an adult."

It is vital to not let these little power moves fool you. While you might want to bow down and respect your boss, you should not let intimidation enter the relationship. Otherwise, you will bend over backward to do whatever he wants, no matter how much it violates your personal ethics and morals or your boundaries. Stay late and miss your child's recital? Sure! Stay all weekend and miss that concert you've been looking forward to? Sure! Shred the documents before the IRS audit? Well, OK. You become compliant to the wrong things and let your boss push you around.

The key instead is to respect his authority. Always address him the way he wants to be addressed – by his first name, sir, whatever he tells you. Then you must comply with what you must to keep your job. But when it comes to bullying, just look him right back in the eyes and say, "No, I can't." Stand up for yourself from early on to prove that you are not a pushover who is awed by his little bit of power.

The same principle works for cops and other such authorities. An example is a cop who attempts to bully you into letting him into your house without a search warrant. His gun and his stature are threatening and you are tempted to comply. But by standing your ground, you are within your legal rights and nothing can really happen.

You will find that standing up to intimidation works really well in most cases. People don't push their authority too much past the image. But in some cases, it doesn't work well at all. Some people get downright scary when their authority is challenged. In this case, you may want to start hunting for a new job, or try to compromise with your boss to avoid having your boundaries hurt. Just don't let this job make you feel that you have to sell your soul to the devil in order to keep making money. If your boss fires you over saying no, or a co-worker tries to get you fired, you can find other jobs – even with a bad reference from this one! Don't let your boss threaten you into thinking that you can't say no and you can't leave if you want to.

Triangulation

Some petty manipulation also often goes on within the office setting. These are little manipulation tactics that are often used by co-workers rather than bosses, though bosses may play into them as well. People use these to create drama and conflict in the office to bully you, emotionally manipulate you, and get you to do what they want. Ignoring or disabling these games will get you far.

One major petty game involves triangulation. This is where a person tells you, "Susie said you always mess up the fax reports." Then you get mad at Susie and say, "I don't, she's the one who doesn't understand how the reports should look." Then the office triangulator runs back to Susie and repeats what you said so that Susie is mad at you now. This creates a schism between you and Susie, when neither of you had a problem before.

The office gossip will also repeat things you said, but he or she may twist the words to make you look worse. He or she may plant total lies about you or focus on your flaws simply to lower your esteem in the eyes of other co-workers.

The best way to answer all of these pathetic power ploys is to ignore them. When somebody tries to triangulate, say, "Why did Susie feel comfortable telling you that?" This tells the triangulator that you know his or her game and you're not playing it. He or she will back off.

When someone spreads lies about you, he or she expects you to get very defensive. Avoid that reaction. Act as if you haven't heard the rumors. When someone asks you about it, just matter-of-factly state the truth, without speaking ill of the gossip. That makes you look good and clears your reputation. Speaking ill of the manipulator puts you on his or her level, which is what he or she wants.

When someone misrepresents your words, you may politely correct him or her in front of everyone else. "Hey, Mike, I heard you misunderstood me earlier. I said I was going to work late, not that I hate working late. Thanks!" Doing this cheerfully without a hint of anger or defensiveness will totally disarm the manipulator. Plus, it will clear your name and tell the whole office the truth. It will even embarrass the manipulator in a way that he or she can't reasonably get mad about without looking terrible to everyone else.

Don't give into the manipulator by acting out or you will look bad and possibly earn points against your employment future, regardless of how poor the manipulator behaves. The manipulator will always win if you play his or her games and act out emotionally. This means that you can't take part in triangulation, repeat gossip, call names back, or have an emotional shouting match or meltdown in front of other people. You can't confront the manipulator in an angry way, either.

Be sure to keep a password-protected log of all such harassment. HR may not be helpful – but they may be. Having a log can help you stand up for yourself should your job become threatened by a very manipulative and vindictive person. Keeping your nose clean, staying uninvolved in office drama, and never repeating gossip or taking part in triangulation will further improve your reputation so that you look even better as you fight for your job.

Being Conditioned To Accept Harassment

Conditioning can involve repeated exposures to the same stimulus until you don't notice it anymore, and instead respond the way the manipulator wants. While conditioning can be used to train a person to perform actions in response to stimulus, it can also be used to desensitize a person so that the manipulator can get away with what he wants [12]. Basically, if you don't get angry, you get a positive reward, like fitting in or getting praised. These things cause you to start to turn the other cheek to offenses on the workplace, even if you don't agree with them at all.

Take sexual harassment. You are a new woman in the office and you respect yourself. Yet when the men there say sexist or suggestive things and you get mad, they tell you to stop being so sensitive because that's just how everyone jokes around in the office. In time, you become accustomed to it. The sexual harassment escalates but you don't do anything about it because you have been conditioned to accept it.

This is the scary reality of how some workplaces can become so terrible in a short amount of time. Horrible jokes, sexual harassment, and other behaviors run rampant and no one says anything at all because the culture of the office has been tempered to allow it by one or more manipulative authorities. This happens in *The Office,* but it is far less humorous in real life.

The best way to change an office's culture is to refuse to jump on the bandwagon and go with the flow. When somebody offends you, confront him or her.

When he or she tells you to lighten up, say that you won't and he or she needs to be mindful of your feelings. People will call you uptight or "not fun" and that is just how they try to make you feel at fault for their own inappropriate behavior. Just sticking up for yourself will empower others and help change the culture around.

Evidence is always critical in these situations. If you can get a recording, HR should be quite interested. Take it to higher-ups in the corporate chain if you must. Escalate the matter until someone does something about it. Legal action may even be appropriate, especially in the case of racial or sexual harassment.

Being Manipulated By A Client

Some clients or customers are great. Others are determined to get their way, no matter what, and they view you as a workhorse, here to do their bidding.

They may move goalposts. This is where they create new expectations of you once you have met the ones they previously set, so that they are never satisfied and your work is never good enough. This game is best handled by making the terms and expectations very clear from the get-go. When they attempt to change them, say, "I'm sorry, but that wasn't in the original contract." Having everything in writing will protect you.

They may also use guilt to make you feel as if you need to give them the moon. Make your terms and promises clear and realistic. Explain why you can't do more. Refuse to let them bully you into extra work or unreasonable deadlines. Try to frame it in a way that benefits them: "To give you the best quality, I can't possibly have this done in two days. I need more time to create a perfect project for you."

Almost all pushy people are entirely self-absorbed so

you can spin things in a way that focus on what will benefit them. This is a low-level form of manipulation that works on most people, particularly those in power or those who are pushy and selfish. Never talk about yourself; focus on the reward they will get by giving you what you want. People like positive rewards and will respond to them [12].

Clients may also pretend to be shopping around for a deal. They may not be doing this, or they may be doing it. That doesn't matter. What matters is that they are seeking to get you to feel a sense of urgency and lower your price just to keep them around. The more you do that, though, the less respect you gain from your clients. To get good, loyal clients, you really must be respectable. The best way to do this is to stick to your guns and never offer deals. Don't let clients pressure you into feeling that you must make a great deal in order to beat the competition. Doing so makes you look desperate and like a pushover.

Clients like to take you out of your home court by proposing meetings in places where you are not familiar. This makes you more uncomfortable and vulnerable, so that you give in to their demands more easily. Therefore, avoid this by always having meetings in your office or a place you are comfortable in. Keep it in your court. This gives you an advantage and helps you stick to your guns.

You should always use commitment and consistency [1]. This builds brand loyalty. People tend to stick with what they know. Clients are more willing to keep paying money to the brand or company that they trust than changing companies. They will only change if they feel it is best. Delivering familiarity and using familiarity in meetings can help set them at ease, letting them know that they are wise to stick with you.

Sometimes, a client may threaten to terminate the contract just to get you to cave. He is using pressure to get you to bend to his will. The best way to go about this is to flatter him and then tell him that you understand if he must move on to another company. The client will be shocked that you value his business yet don't really care if he moves on. He won't feel as if you are easily bullied anymore.

Being Manipulated By Your Boss

When I was a video clerk in high school, my boss came in one day and told me, "We caught you doing something on camera. What do you think it was?" I freaked out and tried to think of anything bad I had done. "I was flirting with that girl?" I asked with a tremor in my voice.

Then my boss laughed and assured me that he was just tricking me. "We caught someone stealing." He laid photos on the counter. And I felt sick to my stomach. Though I had done nothing wrong, he had tricked me into telling him something anyway. I could have gotten myself into trouble.

The lesson here is that you should never let your boss trick you in this way. Don't admit to any wrongdoing unless directly accused with evidence. Usually, it's your word against someone else's and standing your ground and keeping your story straight will save you.

Your boss may also use guilt to make you feel as if you must put in more effort, stay later, etc. As you see him sitting in his office way past dark, you feel inclined to do this as well. He is great at leading you to do what he wants without directly asking. This is a trait of a good boss who knows how to use manipulation in his position of power, but it is also bad for you because you have less autonomy. When you feel guilty, remind yourself of all that you have done for the company to soothe your emotions. Make a logical decision as opposed to an emotional one about whether or not to stay late, take on another project, or whatever it is you feel pressures to do.

Bosses are very adept at FOG. They can make you fear that you might lose your job and not get a good reference, so they use that power to make you do what they want. Then they use obligation to make you feel that you must do things to avoid losing your job and to please your boss, who is your authority after all. Finally, they use guilt to make you feel further obligated. The thing is, most of the time your job is safer than you think because the company would rather keep you than invest money in hiring and training a new employee. While this isn't always the case, it usually is. So do good work but don't let your boss wring everything out of you. You can say no.

When going up against your boss, you must always flatter his job and his position to stroke his ego. Then you must present your case and how it will benefit him. For instance, "I admire your commitment to this deadline and getting this project done tonight. I think I should go home now, though, so that I can be well-rested and perform at my best at the client meeting tomorrow." That sounds better than, "Why do you want me to stay late? I'm really tired and the game is on!

Chapter 7: Specific Considerations For Manipulation

In Other Areas Of Life

Manipulation is everywhere. Salespeople attempt to manipulate you to buy new cars and furniture, marketing manipulates you to feel bad about yourself so you try a new product or service, family manipulates you to come out for Thanksgiving when you don't feel like it, and friends manipulate you to babysit or pick sides during a friend-fight. All of these people working at you can make you feel crazy, as if you have no real say in your own life. That's why learning to identify, block, and even reverse manipulation in the more personal areas of life can make a big difference in your self-esteem and peace of mind. Gain more autonomy by blocking manipulation from your own loved ones.

Family

Family may just be the most manipulative people of

all. You never know who you are thrown in with – you didn't pick your family. But as you grow up together, you tend to get used to, and thus look past, each other's individual personality traits and flaws. The result is that you may tolerate behavior from your Aunt Sarah that you would never tolerate from anyone else. You may even be flabbergasted at times by how your family members behave.

Families tend to have hierarchies just like any group of human beings do. Your place in the hierarchy is pretty static by now. Some people may feel that they have dominance over you and can push you around or manipulate you as they choose. As you attempt to use the skills in this book, your efforts to gain proper treatment can be quite unwelcome. Learning how to crumble this resistance by simply standing your ground and refusing to back down is imperative to change anything within your family dynamic.

The Guilt Trip

Many family members will try to make you feel guilty to get their way and make excuses for how they treat you. An abusive father might say that you wouldn't listen so he had to resort to threats and hitting. An abusive mother might complain that you don't do anything for her when you are visiting her at her home every day and trying your best to care for her. Meddling family members who spread rumors about you, family members who lie to you and steal from you, and family members who go to great lengths to enable and protect addicts who have hurt the rest of the family are all abusive in their own way. They tend to use guilt as their favorite weapon,

It is best to understand that you are your own person, whether your family likes it or not. You have a right to set boundaries, to stand up for yourself, and to make your own decisions. When your family calls you irresponsible, selfish, mean, or a million other things, it is best to not believe it.

When someone starts to use guilt trips on you, be

sure to present a list of things you have done right. You may also offer an apology and then request that you talk about something else. Changing the subject can help you avoid accountability [1].

Refusing Accountability

One of the most common tactics that abusers employ within families is refusing to take accountability for any wrongdoing, including past child abuse. If your parents or older siblings were abusive and you confront them, you are likely to be made into the bad guy. The same scenario plays out between generations and all family members as the ones who are truly in the wrong refuse to say sorry.

The best bet here is to stop hoping for miracles. Family members who don't apologize to you will never see the errors of their ways, no matter how awful they were to you. Holding them accountable verbally only sets you up to get hurt. It is far better to put as much distance as you can from them and work on forgiving them for your own sake.

When a family member won't apologize, you can start the healing process by sending him or her a letter. That prevents the discussion from going south and helps you get everything out before the family member can cut you off and argue with you. Nevertheless, you can never expect a true, heartfelt apology.

You cannot change abusers or manipulators. Most of them refuse to admit that they are wrong. Instead, you must focus on reducing the dialogue that you now have with yourself, where you repeat your abuser's words and convince yourself that you are not good enough. You have to learn to love yourself, without the abuser's love. Often it is easiest to heal without being near the abuser, so that you can turn off that toxic dialogue.

Avoid Triangulation

Perhaps the most insidious form of family manipulation is triangulation. You tell your aunt something about your sister and ten minutes later, the whole family is calling you to berate you for what you said and now your sister isn't speaking to you for a year.

After a time or two of this, you can start to learn who the big triangulators are. These are essentially gossips who love to stir up trouble in the family. It is often best to avoid speaking to them, as any information you give them can be used against you.

You should also go directly to other family members to clear your name. This way, you have a chance to explain yourself and end the triangulation before more drama starts. If your family members don't believe you, then just say that you're sorry this happened and you hope that they can eventually move past this.

Find Allies

As you begin to realize that you may be the victim of manipulation, you should reach out to other family members who appear to be victims. Here is how to tell who may be in the same boat as you:

1. They are the center of every conversation; they are the ones who everyone else blames for being wrong.

2. They avoid family functions and keep to themselves. You seldom hear from them, except perhaps through Christmas cards.

3. They attend family functions but they stay quiet. Despite not doing anything, they quickly get blamed for something. People talk about them a lot and the gossip appears to be unwarranted.

4. They are black sheep. They don't act like everyone else. Most of the family hates them for not fitting into the mold.

It is wise to reach out to these people. Calmly mention that you feel something is dysfunctional within the family and you want some help. Ask them if they feel victimized by certain family members as well.

When you find out that you are not alone in your family, you can feel better with allies. You can also fortify yourself with these allies at family functions. It is always easier to stick up for yourself with a friend at your side [13].

Having a friend can also help you see through gaslighting. When a family member attempts to deny or alter reality to you, you have someone else to keep you grounded and sure of your perception. Don't ever let family gaslight you. Always keep your bearings about you. Recording conversations discreetly on your phone may be ideal if you can't have your supportive family with you.

Break The Patterns

Every Thanksgiving, your aunt Carol starts a racist rant until the younger people or the person in a biracial marriage gets angry and blows up at her. Then she acts hurt and complains about how no one has free speech these days. That is a pattern that Aunt Carol relies on to stir up trouble.

Your mom asks you to do something. When you do it, it's not good enough. She yells at you for being a bad child and you walk away feeling terrible about yourself. That is another pattern that she relies on to break down your self-esteem.

Your sister starts her usual criticism of you. When you finally snap and yell at her, the whole family jumps to her defense. "She was only trying to help," they all say. Your sister becomes the center of attention and you look like a bad person, as usual. Your sister uses this pattern to distract from her problems and look like an angel to the family.

Most family manipulation uses patterns to keep behavior going in the same vein. The manipulator relies on these patterns to hurt others' feelings and get the reactions she or he wants. The best thing to do is to identify these patterns and break them before they continue. Stop responding the same way; in fact, try to stop responding at all. Stop engaging in the same arguments and saying the same things. This will throw the family manipulators off.

Stop Going To Functions That Weaken You

When your manipulative mother has you come over when all of her bridge partners and sisters are present, she is bringing you into her court. Everyone is on her side and will defend you if they can. Therefore, you are powerless. It may be best to avoid meeting the family manipulator in a situation where he or she is bolstered by supporters and able to weaken you.

During big family functions, like Christmas dinner, reunions, or other events, it may be best to stay with your "family friends." These are the people who support you and are loving toward you. Smile and say hello to the manipulator(s) to avoid being talked about, but keep your distance. Certainly don't get reeled into a conversation where you are forced to divulge any of your personal details.

Use Your Own Persuasion

To normalize or at least neutralize relations with family, you may consider running your own manipulation.

First, set the stage [5]. You can do this by always being friendly and polite and calm. You can also do this by refusing to follow old patterns of abuse that your family throws at you.

Then start to set your family up using leading questions. "You are a nice person, right?" is one way to make your family members pre-disposed to being nice, just to prove themselves to you. "You want this to be a great night?" is another way.

You can further prime the stage by talking about positive things. This will set everyone's minds in a more positive state, leading to more positive conversations. Should they become negative, you can leave the situation, to condition them to accept that they need to talk nicely around you.

Don't engage in the games, like triangulation. Being like your family and using reverse manipulation on them will only bury you in more drama. The more effective approach is to simply stop taking part in their games and keeping your nose clean. If you have done nothing wrong, then you have far less to fear because your family can't "get" you on anything.

Refuse To Be An Enabler

If you have a drug addict or some other type of addict within your family, then you know how it feels to be manipulated day in and day out. You have made to be a victim of guilt, as your addict family member sobs on the phone until you lend him or her money. You have possibly been robbed and swindled. Your family member keeps promising to get sober...and then never does. The entire family grieves as they watch this person make more and more of a mess of his or her life.

Addiction can make people big manipulators because they live for their addiction of choice. They are not able to see how they hurt others, or when they do see it, they refuse to do anything about it. They are deceptive, partly because they are ashamed of what they are doing and partly because they want to make you think they are fine so that you keep helping them. Often, they start with the best intentions, which their addictions corrode over time.

Most people who deal with addict family members are torn because they don't know how to respond properly. They want to help and they fear the family member may die. But they also don't want to be hurt anymore. As a result, they become enablers, who provide a safe space for the addict to continue with his or her addiction.

Tough love has been shown to work the best time and again, especially on shows like Intervention [14]. In other words, stop being an enabler. Only when you refuse to enable someone's behavior and set firm boundaries do you force the addict to finally change. The addict cannot possibly keep supporting his or her habit, so he or she relents and gets help.

The first step is to take a love-first approach. Always tell the addict that you love him or her and why you love him or her. Many addicts struggle with severe self-esteem issues, so making your love known can be helpful. Then go on to list grievances and ways the addict has hurt you. Conclude with "I can no longer help you."

No contact can also be a good strategy in the case of someone who refuses to change after many promises to the contrary. You may want to simply stop talking to this person or letting him or her into your home. As hurtful as this can be, it protects you. The addict may have other enablers in his or her life, which is why you cannot make a difference by showing tough love. By withdrawing your connection, however, you make an impression that may or may not motivate him or her to change. The key here is to look out for yourself instead of taking care of the addict. It is emotionally harrowing for most people, but it is the only wise course of action after a certain point.

Change must come from within the addict's heart. Forcing him or her to change will only bring you great disappointment. You can foster an environment of change, but you cannot force an addict to do anything. The addict will only make the change when he or she is truly ready. That is a journey of his or her own, which you can only be a supporting part of. One way to offer the most support to stop enabling and protecting the addict from the consequences of his or her problem.

When The Parent-Child Relationship Is Reversed

In normal family dynamics, the parent is the mature, responsible adult and the child gets to play and grow up. But sadly, not all families are like this. In some dysfunctional families, the children must take care of the parents, which robs them of a childhood. Often, in these circumstances, the parents are in fact addicts or extremely young. They are not capable of proper parenting.

Children are easier to manipulate, so parents in this dynamic will do so. As you grow into an adult, you may see that this dynamic is weird and unhealthy. Yet you are still under the spell of your parent's manipulation. You feel too guilty to stop caring for the adult.

The same dynamic may occur with other family members. They are adults but you still feel the need to care for them. This may extend to a sibling or any other family member who needs lots of care, as if he or she is still a young child.

This is where you need to use tough love as well [14]. When an adult needs too much care, it is time to withdraw your support. Recognize the times when you feel guilty and the urge to support or care for this person arises within you. Write it down in a journal. Then redirect that urge and that guilt. Remind yourself that this person is now an adult and needs to learn to care for him- or herself. In the case of parents who act like this, remind yourself that the roles should be reversed.

Taking a break from the relationship can be helpful. Maybe go on a trip or move a little ways away. This helps you become less involved in caring for the adult, without totally severing your relationship. You can still offer support and have a connection with this person, you just can't play Mommy or Daddy anymore.

Romantic Relationships

Manipulation is a common form of abuse in relationships and can often be worsened when you grew up with a manipulative family [15]. The more you encounter this abuse, the more accustomed you become to it, until you stop fighting and become lost in FOG [3]. FOG makes you refuse to leave the relationship and get lost in your ideas of what you must do for this person. It also erodes your sense of self and your reality.

Reaction Formation And Validating Emotions

The cycle that leads to reaction formation is a long one [16]. Reaction formation is a manifestation of behavior that is the opposite of how you really feel. In the case of dealing with manipulators, you may start by being overly affectionate and accommodating when really you feel sick and resentful. You do this to placate the true feelings you have, which are at distinct odds with how you think you should feel. The manipulator preys on this.

You start by wanting to appear kind and loved, so you make it easy for someone to need you. You feel that you are a good person for taking care of someone and noticing the best in him or her when no one else does. Then you learn that you are being used, so you become furious. You feel guilty for this dark emotion, since it is at odds with the kind persona you want to exude, so you do even more for the manipulator just to make yourself feel better. This cycle gets tighter and more vicious, as you become a servant to a person who doesn't even value your humanity.

Manipulators are willing to milk your reaction formation as long as possible until you have enough and stop serving them.

The best way to break this cycle is to set boundaries and refuse to be used. Realize that you are not here to serve or take care of this person, but to be with him or her. A healthy relationship is not at all like the one between a parent and child or nurse and patient. If you feel used, say something and even leave if you must. Don't feel guilty about your own emotions; you have the right to feel what you feel. If you feel used, then you are. Don't dismiss it as paranoia or call yourself a bad person for not wanting to serve your lover, because that's not your job.

Another step is realizing that your emotions are not wrong. If you feel some way, it is your gut telling you a fact about your life. The key here is to listen to and observe these emotions without judging yourself. Ask yourself why you feel this way and review the recent events in your life. Look at how the manipulator treats you. Pay special attention to moments when this anger or resentment peaks and notice what happens then. All of these observations will help you see what you are truly reacting to and then you can accept that your emotions are valid. That way, you can take the appropriate action, such as leaving the toxic relationship or setting firmer boundaries, as opposed to letting your darker feelings manifest in an unhealthy way in a reaction formation [16].

Molding Reality

A lot of manipulators will attempt to mold your reality [17]. They do this by priming you with certain references or exposing you to certain ideas to put your mind on a certain track [5]. A study showed that priming test subjects with words that reminded them of elderly people, such as wrinkles or Florida, made them walk more slowly [19]. This fascinating example shows how people tend to rub off on you with what they say. But manipulators do this more than most, which is why their words can be "sticky." They make more of an impression and more of a difference in your thinking than most people, which is why they can be so infiltrating and addicting in relationships.

Then they will challenge your sense of reality by lying, gaslighting, and twisting the truth so that you feel wrong for how you see things. They will make themselves the victims, as well, when in fact you are the victim. This keeps you from seeing what is real and how the relationship really is. For a long time, you may have your suspicions, but you can never confirm them. The relationship goes on and you are being mistreated without really realizing it or deciding to leave.

Watch out for someone who always challenges your beliefs or denies reality. Also watch out for someone who somehow always makes everything your fault and makes you feel guilty when you bring up an issue. Finally, watch out for people who isolate you, because they are stripping away your bearings so that they can totally infiltrate and alter your perception of reality. All of these things are signs that your reality is being distorted.

Pressure Liars Into The Truth

A liar will evade the truth under any circumstances. A cheater will evade it until he can't anymore, then he will make up some reason why he did it which puts you at fault. Liars and cheaters are running the same game: They are avoiding taking accountability for their own abhorrent actions.

The best way to deal with these cowardly types is to pressure them into the truth. You keep asking the same question over and over. As they attempt to deflect the attention away from themselves by changing the subject or otherwise diverting your mind from the issue at hand, refuse to follow their thinking. Just keep asking your question until you get an answer.

You may also consider laying out the truth before them without saying anything. Leave a print out of texts between your partner and his cheating partner, for instance. Let him explain it and chances are, you will catch him in a lie. Not all manipulators are good liars; they just think they are and they are good at pressuring you into accepting what they say.

Set Boundaries

As a relationship forms, it is influenced by the boundaries you set. Say someone starts calling you at two in the morning for rides after drinking and you happily oblige every time. You just let that person know that it is not only OK to drink as much as he or she wants, but that your sleep time is not important and he or she can intrude. Or say that your partner starts to fight with you about your ex, whom you are totally over. By giving into the fight and assuring this person that you are not still in love with your ex, you tell him or her that it is OK to discuss that.

When a partner exhibits behavior that you don't like the first time, you should say something. This is not a cue to run because everyone makes mistakes. But you really need to let him or her know, "This is not acceptable in the future. I will entertain it now, but not again." Should the person try testing your boundaries on this issue again, you can refuse to get involved or to allow the behavior.

That is how you set boundaries in a relationship. It is crucial from day one. Get to know what you like and don't like based on past relationships. From there, you can surmise the boundaries you should set for this one to work. Remember, you have the right to boundaries. Your happiness is just as important as your partner's. Don't let him or her run over your boundaries as if your happiness does not matter as much.

Most people will test boundaries once or twice and then accept them. A manipulator will continue to push them and even try to convince you to drop certain boundaries. He or she may tell you that you are unreasonable or selfish, or that he or she deserves better. He or she may try to bribe you with a reward, like sex or a massage, if you do one last favor. Don't let these things make you drop your boundaries. The key here is to defend yourself. The more you allow the manipulator to win, the more he or she will violate you in the future.

Don't Permit Social Isolation

A manipulator with controlling and abusive tendencies will attempt to isolate you. This person will accomplish this in one of two ways. The first way is that he or she will permit you to see your family and friends, as if he or she doesn't mind you having a life outside of the relationship. However, he or she will then throw fits, call you constantly, or do other things so that you don't enjoy your time away. Your family and friends feel put off and spend less time with you. If they come over and he is there, he or she will make it so unbearable that they all want to leave.

The second version is that he or she will bad mouth your friends and family. He or she may point out little things they do wrong and blow them out of proportion so that you start to resent your family and friends. Soon, you dislike everyone you used to know and your relationships become strained. Next thing you know, you don't have anyone to talk to besides your partner.

These two scenarios are how manipulators subtly isolate you. Then you are less likely to leave because you feel lonely and dependent on your significant other. Plus, you feel less than good about yourself since you have no one in your life. And finally, you have no one to anchor your sense of reality or protect you from abuse.

When you feel that someone is isolating you, set firm boundaries. It is OK to say, "Don't call while I'm with my friends." It is also OK to say, "These are my friends. Please don't speak badly about them." See if your partner respects that or not. If he or she does not, then it may be time to move on. You should never be isolated by a romantic partner if you want a healthy, normal relationship.

Confront Passive-Aggressive Behavior Head-On

As discussed in Chapter 1, some manipulators just don't know how to communicate. They are scared to speak up so they use passive-aggressive behavior to get their way instead. There is no need to tolerate this in an adult relationship, however.

An example is when you ask your boyfriend to join you at a party that is really important to your friend. He agrees and comes along, making you feel as if you are not being isolated. However, he spends the whole time moping on the couch, making everyone uncomfortable with his negative energy. Your friends even comment that he's being a real downer. You ask him what's wrong and he says, "You know I'm not a party person. Why did you drag me to this thing?" You instantly feel guilty for making him come, so you leave with him and let your friend down. Not only does this hurt your friendship, but it causes you to harbor resentment against your boyfriend for even agreeing to come in the first place.

When a romantic partner pulls a stunt like this, you need to confront the behavior directly. "You said that you wanted to come." Then refuse to give him what he wants. Instead of leaving early, ignore him the rest of the night. Or, tell him he can get a cab home but you're staying. By not playing the game, you let the partner know that this passive aggressive manipulation is not permitted.

Let's consider another form of this manipulation. You ask your girlfriend to watch your dog while you go away. She says yes, but acts as if it's the biggest burden in the world. She rolls her eyes a lot and doesn't do a good job. When you call, she complains constantly about how much the dog sheds and how she hates taking him out. Her whole game is to make you feel guilty for asking something of her.

Again, confront it head-on. Say, "You should have told me you didn't want to take care of my dog so I could have found someone else to do it. I expect better communication." Confrontation like this sets boundaries but also lets the manipulator know that this behavior is not healthy or necessary.

End Rumor Spreading

You think things are going well. Then you find out that the person you're dating has been telling his or her friends that you're a terrible person. They all dislike you now. When you get into a normal fight with your partner, everyone blames you. When you find out your partner is cheating, they all think you deserve it.

When a manipulator makes everyone hate you, he is protecting himself from looking like the bad guy. He is setting the board game up so that no one can fault him. He will make you look crazy in front of others by provoking you into an emotional outburst, he will exaggerate your mistakes and flaws, and he will even make up outright lies. If you confide anything in him, he ensures that everyone knows so that you look bad.

There is no excuse for this to happen. A romantic partner should not smear your reputation to everyone. This is a major red flag that emotional abuse is going on or is about to go on. You should get out now. Nothing makes up for this and no excuse excuses it.

Don't Allow Ex Smearing

When a relationship ends badly, it is normal for one

or both parties to be bitter. There may be some anger and hurtful words. However, it is a warning sign when someone you start dating has something bad to say about every ex of his. This shows that he or she can't take accountability for the dissolution of relationships and will talk badly about you once your relationship ends, as well.

A mature person can admit what he or she did wrong as well. The fault is not all on the other party. If your new partner can't do this, then chances are he or she is a manipulator who prefers playing victim to being honest and taking the blame when necessary.

Some discernment is in order here. Say your partner's ex did something really horrible to him or her. He or she may not be able to say anything nice and may not need to take responsibility since it is not his or hers to bear. However, it is a red flag when a person hates every single one of his or her exes and seems to repeat the same mistakes over and over.

Allow Some Dominance

In Robert Greene's *48 Laws of Power,* the very first rule is to never outshine your master [19]. This can apply in a workplace scenario – your boss hates it if you outshine him in a meeting. But it can also apply in a romantic setting. In every relationship, one person must be dominant. The dominant person will fight for this, either with direct or indirect tactics.

If you are the dominant one, be sure to establish that from day one. It is only fair to your partner to know what he or she is dealing with. But if your partner is the dominant one, it may be best to give him or her that dominance. Fighting for dominance can open up issues and lead to manipulation that is not necessary.

Therefore, don't outshine your partner or intimidate him or her by bragging. Don't fight him or her on every decision. Also don't make decisions without first conferring with him or her. These things will help you establish peace.

Friendships

It is sad when your friends turn out to be manipulators. The people who are supposed to be your number one fans can be working against you secretly. The joke that you shouldn't tell others your problems because half of the people don't care and the other half are glad you have them is often true of friends. Even your best friends feel that they are in competition with you and may be secretly trying to hurt you. Or they may be so wrapped up in their own needs and desires that yours don't matter particularly much.

Say Less than Necessary

Another one of Robert Greene's 48 laws of power, it is imperative to say less than necessary [19]. In fact, keeping things on a need-to-know basis is the best way to protect yourself from manipulation and abuse by friends. Until you know a friend truly well and understand his or her intentions, consider him or her an acquaintance and keep things private. Only say what you need to say.

All too often we rush into friendships and attempt to share all. Then we are shocked when we are manipulated and betrayed. Don't take any person too seriously until some time has elapsed.

Don't Fall For The Victim Game

You have already read about how manipulators play the victim to avoid accountability. A friend is likely to do this. A friend who can't say sorry is not a real friend at all. Don't expect much from him or her.

A friend who makes you feel guilty or sorry for her is most likely a manipulator. She is setting up herself as a victim so that you don't ever hold her accountable.

She is also playing with your emotions so that you do things for her.

Watch Out For Fairweather Friends

Does your friend only call when she needs something? Does he only want to hang out when you are doing well in life, yet disappears when you are in need? Does your friend tune out as you speak? All of these are hallmarks of a fake and shallow friend who isn't truly there for you. This friend only wants you when you have something to give.

Over time, a friend's patterns of behavior can reveal a lot about his or her intentions. Fair-weather friends are ones who aren't there for you yet expect you to be there for them. They are sneakily awful because they pretend to be your friend without giving you any benefits.

Watch Out For Gossips

The friend who has nothing nice to say, who gossips about your other friends, and who criticizes you is not just blunt. He or she may say "I'm just blunt and no one likes it," but the truth is, he or she is just hurtful and rude. People with nothing nice to say are running a constant critique in their minds. They are criticizing and complaining about you, too, behind your back.

Don't Do Too Many Favors

A friend may ask you a small favor, like to help her with her laundry. Then you discover that months later, you are still doing her laundry for her and she does nothing for you. Or a small request for twenty bucks may turn into a much larger loan. Friends are free to ask for favors – that's what friends are for. But the friend who always asks for favors and never reciprocates is a user.

Don't allow this to go on too long. Be assertive and

say when enough is enough. Also feel free to say no when someone is asking too much of you. No friend is worth overextending yourself.

Also don't allow a friend to do lots of favors for you. He or she may be doing nice things that you don't ask for in order to make you owe him or her. Later, this person will collect. He or she is operating on the Principle of Reciprocity [1].

The Friend Who Flakes

A friend who says she's busy, only to be spotted at the mall with someone else, likely uses people. She has a network of friends and spends time with whoever serves her the best. She does not view you as a friend, but rather as an accessory that she can pick up and use as she sees fit.

It is best to note when people flake on you only to spend time with others. If a friend doesn't seem to enjoy your company, chances are he or she is only using you when convenient. Feeling like you are the subpar or least favorite friend is a sign that this is happening. Another sign is when this friend calls you when he or she needs something, yet seems to forget your existence when he or she has a party.

Chapter 8: How To Stop Being Manipulated By Money

Since money makes the world go around, it makes sense that a lot of people can be manipulated by it. The key to avoiding financial abuse or manipulation is to stop relying so heavily on another's money.

Money is a great way for people to manipulate you. Your parents might promise to send a monthly stipend...if you do everything perfectly, take the classes they want, and prove that you are making only the best grades. Your partner may pay for everything and then use it as a guilt trip when you bring up problems in the relationship or try to break up. A friend may give you a "gift" and then always hold it over your head so that you feel obligated to do her favors. It is best to avoid these situations.

Is It Worth It?

When someone offers you money, compare that

money to the demands you are facing. A client may be dangling a lot of money over your head that you will never see because his demands are too high. A partner may be willing to pay off your student loans...but he or she owns you and will control your every move.

Before you get involved with someone's money, get to know them better. Get a sense of their reputation by talking to other people who know them. Look into their past and their criminal background. All of these things can help you gauge if this is the right financial relationship.

Above all, listen to your gut. The human brain still has very sharp instincts and can tell when someone is not trustworthy [20]. The key here is to avoid ignoring your own sense. If someone does things you don't really like often, or makes you feel weird, then don't get involved in a financial relationship!

Be Financially Sound Alone

When you are dependent on someone for money, you are in a vulnerable position. Being unemployed leads you to depend on your partner or friend, for instance. This becomes a really sticky situation. It is best to always make sure that you can support yourself on your own. If you can't, start to take the necessary steps to do so.

You can't be as manipulated by money if you don't really need it. Everyone wants more money, but as long as you can survive on your own without the extra cash, you won't be as willing to sell your soul to the devil.

Refuse Gifts

Money should never be a gift, just a loan. If someone insists that he or she just wants to help you out, say no thanks and set clear terms to pay back the loan. When someone gives you a financial gift, they are setting you up to be a major victim in the future. They have something over you that they can use.

In the case that a person refuses repayment, document and record that for the future when this person tries to finagle you to do something for repayment. You may also whip this proof out should this person bring it up in a fight and say, "You can't be mad at me. You never even paid me back that money I lent you!"

Be Private About Money

Manipulators are constantly searching for something to hold over you or some way to get control over you. One way they do this is by acting like kind benefactors when you are in financial dire straits. They overhear you talking about some expensive home improvement project you must perform to escape a code violation, so they swoop in and offer the money. They listen to you lament how you can't leave your abusive husband because you can't afford the deposit on a place so they either give you the deposit or have you move into their home. These people are sharks, circling and looking for a weak point they can exploit.

The first lesson here is to just avoid people who are too generous and too kind. No one in this world is actually altruistic. They all have something to gain from helping you.

The second lesson is to just be more private about your financial situations. There are several reasons that it is a huge faux pas to talk about money issues or discuss how much money you make in public. One such reason is protecting yourself from the sharks.

Don't Let Money Keep You In A Horrid Job

Or a relationship, or any other bad situation. While you may have no choice right now, it is best to start looking for another opportunity so that you can leave your current one gracefully and without too much financial pain. You want to have a new job before you leave your current one, or a new living situation before you bounce on your narcissistic roommate.

Don't let the promise of raises and promotions keep you locked in a job that is unsatisfactory. That raise or promotion may never even come and you slave for it for years. Also, don't stay in a toxic living situation or relationship because the other person helps you save money. People will use money to make a situation seem ideal when really the money is the only good part of it. Life is so much more than money so don't let it blind you.

Chapter 9: No Contact And Preventing Manipulation Right Off The Bat

There is only one tried and true way to kill manipulation: Don't allow it from the beginning by going no contact. This move is not always possible with manipulators you know well, but it is beyond effective for those that have just entered your life.

Prove You're Not A Victim

When you first meet people, you must prove that you are no victim. This entails using a power pose and appearing dominant [10]. Appear taller and make firm eye contact. Don't cross your arms or fidget, or you will give away the fact that you are a pushover.

Just Walk Away

When a person starts acting like a child and manipulating everyone, just roll your eyes, either out loud or in your head, and say, "Oh, children!" That helps you laugh the whole thing off without getting upset. This ploy is great with triangulators, gaslighters, and people who throw fits to get their way. The girl who pouts at a party until her boyfriend leaves is another example.

When a person starts manipulating you, just smile and say, "No." Then turn and walk away. Don't talk to this person again. Don't play games. And certainly, don't let them get to you emotionally and make you feel guilty or otherwise.

You must always stay cool as a cucumber around manipulators. Remember, they are irrational people who are more than willing to get irate. They won't back down if you show the same behavior because they are so comfortable with it. What really freaks them out is when you don't buy into whatever emotional state they are provoking and start crying, yelling, or otherwise making a scene.

The best response to gaslighting is always, "I know what I saw and so do you." Then walk away so that they can't keep arguing. Cutting arguments short is an ideal way to shut down a manipulator. Prove you don't care for being manipulated by refusing to try to win because you won't. You have better things to do.

Don't engage in debates or allow someone to yell at you and berate you. When someone tries to denigrate you, tell them, "I would appreciate it if you stopped talking to me like that." The manipulator may escalate, in which case you should leave the situation. No one can fault you for that.

The True Meaning Of No Contact

No contact is when you simply ghost someone, giving them no explanation, no apology, and no further communication. You just walk away...never to be seen or heard from again. When you see them in public, you may either ignore them completely or say hello politely, but you don't engage in any conversation that may open doors for further manipulation and abuse.

No contact is the best course of action when dealing with emotionally unstable or character-disordered manipulators. These people want to feed off of you to help their own mental issues. Your job is not to be a sponge or a nurse, so you must walk away. Otherwise, they will continue to find ways to make you feel guilty and sucker you in. Narcissists in particular will use you as a supply of ego, so no contact is the only way to truly drive them away.

No contact also helps you avoid the charm or the emotional whirlpool that manipulators use to keep you around. By not talking to them anymore, you can let go of their toxic behavior and influence. Nothing can make you change your mind now.

Many people don't realize that no contact should extend to social media and mutual contacts. Tell people not to talk to you about the person in question, as they can suck you back in as well. Also, block all social media accounts to avoid seeing this person's life and feeling drawn in again. All it takes is one post threatening self-harm, moaning about missing you, or invoking jealousy to get you back into the emotional cycle manipulators like so much.

Conclusion

How does it feel to be manipulation-proof? I'm sure it feels wonderful! Being manipulated makes you feel like pond scum and being able to defeat, deflect, and conquer manipulators is empowering and liberating. Your life will certainly be more enjoyable, now that you can make decisions for yourself and avoid the toxic people who manipulate you.

Manipulation is caused by a variety of underlying communication and mental issues. It is not always the fault of the manipulator. Media portrays all manipulators as horrible people, but this is not always true. Nevertheless, you don't have to stand for it and let someone use you as a pawn. Having to stand up to great people that you love hurts but it is worth it. People must learn to respect you and not use you.

As you get caught up in manipulation, you can find yourself in a vicious cycle. Now you have learned to spot manipulators and victimhood before you get into that cycle, how to weaken and confront manipulators when you are in the cycle, and how to break out of the cycle and heal.

Relationships should be based on healthy communication and choices. Manipulation is a normal human communication tactic, but it should not be abused. If you are being manipulated a lot, you should put an end to it, or to the whole relationship. Prove to others that you are dominant and that you respect yourself too much to be someone else's puppet. If a person wants you to do something, he should ask, and then respect you when you say no.

With the information in this book, you are now able to finally break free of some of this bull. You can mend relationships built on poor communication and low-level manipulation, and evade the higher-level manipulation that is so hurtful and damaging. Life will be better as you can respect yourself, set firm boundaries, and encourage good communication and healthy respect with your peers and loved ones. From the workplace to the bedroom, manipulation is rampant but you are in control of it now!

You have even learned some techniques to combat manipulators effectively. These techniques are a powerful way to assert and gain dominance over others. Watch your relationships improve and your career skyrocket as you employ these tactics. No one will be able to get to you and intimidate you anymore. Your bosses will think that you sure look good as you become the foolproof powerhouse of the office.

Now that you know how to end and combat manipulation, you can have more peaceful relationships that don't tamper with your boundaries. You can also find people who don't test these boundaries. Your self-esteem will soar as a result as you finally get a taste of how healthy relationships work. The load off of your mind when you lose toxic manipulators will be like a breath of fresh air and you will attack life with renewed vigor.

It is time to start renovating your life with what you have learned in this book. You should reread it whenever you encounter a new manipulator who is trying to somehow con you. Don't ever put up with it. Just stand up for yourself and get the respect that you deserve!

References

1. Cialdini, Robert. *Harnessing the Science of Persuasion*. Harvard Business Review.

2. Cialdini, R. (2008). *Influence, Science, and Practice, 5th Ed*. Allyn and Bacon. ISBN-13: 978-0205609994.

3. Forward, Susan & Frazier, Donna. (n.d.) *Emotional Blackmail: When the People in Your Life Use Fear, Obligation, and Guilt to Manipulate You*. Harper Paperbacks. ISBN: 978-0060928971.

4. Jonason, Peter & Webster, Gregory. *The Dirty Dozen Scale for Dark Triad Personality Traits*. https://openpsychometrics.org/tests/SD3/.

5. Cialdini, Robert. (2016). *Pre-suasion: A Revolutionary Way to Influence and Persuade*. Simon & Schuster. ASIN: B01C36E2YS.

6. Damasio, H., Damasio, A., Bechara, A. (2006). *Role of the Amygdala in Decision-Making*. Annals of the New York Academy of Sciences. Vol 985, Issue 1.https://doi.org/10.1111/j.1749-6632.2003.tb07094.x.

7. Jung, Nadine, Et Al. (2014). How Emotions Affect Logical Reasoning: Evidence From Experiments With Mood-Manipulated Participants, Spider Phobics, And People With Exam Anxiety. Frontier Psychology, Vol 5, Issue 570, Doi: 10.3389/Fpsyg.2014.00570

8. Cryder, C., Springer, S., & Morewedge, C. (February 2012). *Guilty Feelings, Targeted Actions*. Social Psychology Bulletin, 38:607, DOI: 10.1177/0146167211435796.

9. Moser, Jason, Et Al. (2017). Third-Person Self-Talk Facilitates Emotion Regulation Without Engaging Cognitive Control: Converging Evidence From Erp And Fmri. Science Report. Vol 17, P. 4519. Doi: 10.1038/S41598-017-04047-3

10. Carney, DR., Cuddy, A., & Yap, A. (2010). *Power Posing: Brief Nonverbal Displays Affect Neuroendocrine Levels and Risk Tolerance.* Psychological Science, Vol 1-6, DOI: 10.1177/0956797610383437

11. Chan, E. & Sengupta, J. (2010). *Insincere Flattery Actually Works: A Dual Attitudes Perspective.*

Journal of Marketing Research, Vol. 41, Issue 1, DOI: https://doi.org/10.1509/jmkr.47.1.122.

12. Herrnstein, R.J. (1990). *Behavior, Reinforcement, and Utility.* Psychological Science. Vol 1, Issue 4, https://doi.org/10.1111/j.1467-9280.1990.tb00203.x.

13. Friedman, Ann. (2013). *Shine Theory: Why Powerful Women Make the Greatest Friends.* The New York Times. https://www.thecut.com/2013/05/shine-theory-how-to-stop-female-competition.html.

14. Hazelden Betty Ford. (2019). *How to Do an Intervention.* https://www.hazeldenbettyford.org/addiction/intervention/how-to-do-an-intervention.

15. Walker, Lenore. (1979). *The Cycle of Violence.* http://www.bdvs.org.au/resource_files/bdvas/IR_5_Cycle-of-violence-factsheet.pdf

16. Reaction Formation. (n.d.). *Merriam-Webster.* https://www.merriam-webster.com/medical/reaction%20formation.

17. Kolenda, Nick. *Methods of Persuasion: How to Use Psychology to Influence Human Behavior.* Kolenda Entertainment. ISBN-13: 978-0615815657.

18. Kahneman, Daniel. (2011). *Thinking Fast and Slow.* Farrar, Straus and Giroux. ASIN: B00555X8OA.

19. Greene, Robert & Elfers, Joost. *The 48 Laws of Power.* Penguin Books. ASIN: B0024CEZR6.

20. Goldberg, Sanford. (n.d.) *The Trust Project.* Northwestern Kellogg. https://www.kellogg.northwestern.edu/trust-project/videos/goldberg-ep-1.aspx

Disclaimer

The information contained in this book and its components, is meant to serve as a comprehensive collection of strategies that the author of this book has done research about. Summaries, strategies, tips and tricks are only recommendations by the author, and reading this book will not guarantee that one's results will exactly mirror the author's results.

The author of this book has made all reasonable efforts to provide current and accurate information for the readers of this book. The author and its associates will not be held liable for any unintentional errors or omissions that may be found.

The material in the book may include information by third parties. Third party materials comprise of opinions expressed by their owners. As such, the author of this book does not assume responsibility or liability for any third party material or opinions.

written expressed and signed permission from the author.

Printed in Great Britain
by Amazon